T4-ALB-202

George Caleb Bingham
of Missouri

GEORGE CALEB BINGHAM
of
MISSOURI

The Story of an Artist

BY

ALBERT CHRIST-JANER

With Preface By

THOMAS HART BENTON

Illustrated in color and in black and white

DODD, MEAD & COMPANY

NEW YORK   1 9 4 0

ND
237
B59
C5

Copyright, 1940

By DODD, MEAD AND COMPANY, Inc.

ALL RIGHTS RESERVED
NO PART OF THIS BOOK MAY BE REPRODUCED IN ANY FORM
WITHOUT PERMISSION IN WRITING FROM THE PUBLISHER

PRINTED IN THE UNITED STATES OF AMERICA
BY THE VAIL-BALLOU PRESS, INC., BINGHAMTON, N. Y.

TO

Edward

Victor

Arland

who find steady comfort

in their cause

Preface

WHEN George Caleb Bingham's work was exhibited in New York a few years ago the majority of those who make their living talking about the Arts were inclined to be supercilious. They said Bingham was a backwoods painter, pretty good in Missouri but not worthy of much serious discussion. I expect they are telling a different story now. Bingham is becoming a sort of national figure and even quite "arty" critics are conceding his technical capacities.

To the intelligent layman it must seem odd the way judgments turn in the consideration of works of art—the way they reverse themselves and declare good what yesterday was thought bad. And yet it is not so strange. Judgments are conditioned by habits and the defense of these. Most aesthetic judgments, like those of the political and economic world, are determined not by facts but by verbal usage, by word forms which are patterned to describe things and ways which one has learned to like and to which one's ego has become attached. These become habitual and when something comes along which fails to be enclosed by them it is quite natural that it should be frowned upon or treated with contempt. Linguistic descriptive patterns have tremendous stultifying effects in all life. It is not extraordinary that they should nearly dominate the field of aesthetic judgment.

Our critics of the last few decades, like our artists, have been trained to see the values of painting and to form their judgments about it on the particular technical ways and subject trends of modern French painting. Modern French painting is all right; it has produced many beautiful and interesting things, fully worthy of admiration, but it has also set up response habits among our artistic authorities which have worked against a free approach to other art forms. These habits, objectified in numerous critical and appreciative essays, have crystallized into standards which, while they may be effective momentarily for the French painting responsible for them, have little or no validity when applied to other kinds. An unending procession of verbal structures strung around such terms as "significant form" and "functional color" have followed the last few decades of French experiment in painting. While, as just indicated, these may have some validity in reference to the particularities of that painting, they cease to be useful for periods in which painting operated under other concepts. There is something grossly absurd in the current habit of testing the Florentine masters or the little Dutch painters by conceptions growing out of impressionism or the technical frustrations of an artist like Cézanne.

The involved analyses which have piled up around the minute details of Cézanne's technique cannot be applied universally. To my mind it is doubtful whether they have, even with regard to Cézanne, more than the passing value of intellectual fads. It is certain they have no significance whatever for estimating the worth of such an artist as George Caleb Bingham.

Bingham lived in a day when it was the picture rather than the way it was made which occupied the amateur's attention. No elaborate pseudo-technical verbiage was erected between his pictures and his audience. If he painted a tree, it was a tree and not a sign pointing to some obscure world of special values with which this cult or that was trying to prove its superior sensibility. Painting was plainer and more matter of fact in Bingham's days. There were no painters' painters nor was one supposed to need some special training or some occult capacity to determine whether or not one liked an artist's work. A picture was not directed to coteries of precious experts but to ordinary people who might buy it and put it in their homes. This was healthy and as it should be and, though Bingham lived in a world which was still close to the wilderness and faced hard times now and then, he had a public and was a successful artist. He painted for a living world and painted what that world could understand—its own life.

American painting is again coming back to this simplicity. Somehow over the heads of the experts and indifferent to its clash with the imported formulas of the critically élite, American painting is rising again as a popular art, as an art that has meaning for Americans. It is creating a new atmosphere and a growing public, seeing its escape from the hot-houses of borrowed cultivation, is watching it with interest. The daily press and the magazines applaud it and argue about it in terms that plain people can understand. Studies of our American artistic past are being made. Adventurous-minded individuals and even the Federal government have delved into our folk art and found values where values were not even suspected a few years ago.

Just how all this interest has grown and how the stage has been set in the wide-spread appreciation of contemporary American effort of an original sort it would be hard to say. Certainly the aftermath of the great war, the disillusionment with European beliefs and practices had something to do with it. Seeing the bitter fruits of European political and economic thinking, it is as if Americans had become suspicious of the flowers, also, of European poetry and art and were ready to throw them out and try growths of their own. Though this may, and does at times, harden into a narrow and short-sighted nationalism it is, on the whole, salutary. It is breaking down the smug intellectual borrowings of the experts, it is building up an atmosphere where American paintings may be judged by something other than their similarity to the latest importation from Paris.

The Regionalist movements of late years, emotional out-croppings of the South and Middlewest but bolstered, nevertheless, by new findings in anthropology and archaeology, have tended to re-define culture. The basic nature of a true culture as the outgrowth of the pressures of a locality is recognized, and more and more intelligent Americans are questioning the validity of cultural pretensions which lean on borrowed artifacts and conceptions. In this new psychological atmosphere, this study of George Caleb Bingham fits readily. Here is an artist who, though technically allied to the High Renaissance, was able like his great contemporary, Daumier, similarly allied, to direct his procedures to the life he knew. Instead of fitting life to his processes, he fitted these to his life and made thereby a unique and original series of forms.

Artistic techniques, like scientific processes, are universally applicable, but the creative artist is one who sees them simply as instruments and applies them to describing or enclosing his own experiences. Experiences, when they are deep enough to be compelling, have ways of affecting techniques, of modifying them. Out of such modifications, often slight, come the new forms of art and the new meanings. Bingham, without denying or breaking with the great occidental traditions of painting, made a specifically American statement. While the United States will certainly produce greater and more accomplished artists in the future, George Caleb Bingham, out of the valley of the Missouri, must always be remembered as among the first of those who set the pace.

THOMAS HART BENTON

KANSAS CITY, MO.
FEBRUARY, 1940

Foreword

ALTHOUGH there was so much that could properly have been said, little has been written about a man of the genius of George Caleb Bingham. Of course, there have been newspaper and magazine articles on certain phases of the man, his life and work. But up until now, the only real study on the subject is an excellent, but brief, monograph by Miss Fern Rusk.

The present volume by Albert Christ-Janer is both timely and conclusive. It evokes my sincere praise. I feel now that the Bingham I knew and admired for many years has at last been adequately presented within these pages and has at last come into his own. This comprehensive and sympathetic interpretation of a subject dear to my heart will, no doubt, help to acquaint others with the life and work of one too little known, The Missouri Artist: George Caleb Bingham.

C. B. ROLLINS

COLUMBIA, MISSOURI
1940

Introduction

In this volume I have attempted to fulfill three objectives: to analyze and clarify the genre work of George Caleb Bingham by presenting some hitherto unpublished drawings; to throw new light upon the personality and the work of the artist by including a series of recently discovered letters; and to correct some mistaken material heretofore published upon this subject and to amplify, with information gleaned from new sources, the history of the Missouri artist.

It would be impossible to complete a study of Bingham's life and work without the aid of those who, at a time when Americana was not as popular a theme as it is among the writers today, worked to keep alive the name of this nineteenth century "regionalist." And so I feel heavily indebted to Fern Helen Rusk, now Mrs. John Shapley, for the excellent little book written in 1914, *George Caleb Bingham*, which is the foundation upon which this present volume is built. Had Miss Rusk had available the material which has come to light during the past twenty-five years, I am sure the book which I have written would not have been necessary.

I feel a sense of obligation, too, to one of the modern "regionalists," Thomas Hart Benton, who encouraged me to complete this study and who, in his high regard for the traditions of Missouri, approaches the paintings of his predecessor with sympathy and understanding.

Like Miss Rusk, I know that no biography of Bingham could be complete without the help of Mr. C. B. Rollins, of Columbia, Missouri. Because he is a thorough historian and because he is the single living man who intimately knew the artist, Mr. Rollins was able to extend invaluable assistance to me as I, frequently, was confounded by an apparent impasse.

The letters written by George Caleb Bingham to James Sidney Rollins were made available to me by him. The authenticity of innumerable statements in this volume was guaranteed by his word. The completeness of the work was made possible only by his generous contributions. Throughout the past four years Mr. Rollins was intensely interested in assisting me to assemble the truth about Bingham's life and work from all known important sources. My debt is great to this magnanimous friend and adviser.

For permission to photograph the drawings of the figures which Bingham made as preliminary studies for his paintings I am grateful to Mr. W. L. R. Gifford, Librarian, St. Louis Mercantile Library Association. The negatives of a number of the photographs were given me by Mr. James B. Musick, City Art Museum, St. Louis, Missouri. The photographs of the drawings and of some of the paintings were taken by Mr. Paul Parsons of Columbia, Missouri, who, by his expert ability and friendly cooperation, insured a fine quality of illustrative material. For the color plates and for eighteen half tones of drawings, I am obliged to the editors of *Life* Magazine, and especially to Mr. Daniel Longwell and Miss Margit Varga, of the *Life* editorial staff.

To Miss Frances Thompson, Secretary of the Art Department of Stephens College, goes the credit for the discovery of some of the important data won only after patient and sometimes tedious research. For corrections of the manuscript and for suggestions for improvement, I am beholden to Miss Virginia Carpenter, Instructor of Literature, Stephens College.

To Mr. Floyd C. Shoemaker and Mr. Roy King, of The State Historical Society of Missouri, I extend my appreciation for their generosity in giving me the fine cooperation of the Society and its facilities. Permissions to reprint photographs of paintings were granted by The Metropolitan Museum of Art, The William Rockhill Nelson Gallery of Art, The City Art Museum of St. Louis, The State Historical Society of Missouri, Mr. C. B. Rollins, and the St. Louis Mercantile Library Association. Finally, I am aware of the many favors given me by people, too many to name here, whose help added to the completion of this volume and they, knowing who they are, will know too that I am mindful of my obligation to them.

—A<small>LBERT</small> C<small>HRIST</small>-J<small>ANER</small>

CAMBRIDGE, MASS.

FEBRUARY, 1940

Contents

Illustrations

PAINTINGS

[xix]

DRAWINGS

The drawings of the figures contained in the paintings have been inserted in the middle of the volume to facilitate the comparison of these prototypes to the figures which the artist developed in his genre paintings.

George Caleb Bingham
of Missouri

The Historical Background in Missouri

A DEATHLESS saga is yet unsung. It is a saga which, when it is written, will dwarf our present literature with the completeness of its panorama, its vast expanse of time and space. This saga, commemorating the settlement and development of the territory known as the Louisiana Purchase, will not only be picturesque and dramatic, but also intensely vigorous, for it must immortalize that tide of humanity which swept into this huge river basin, bringing with it homesteaders and homes, the lawful and the lawless, those to whom adventure called, and those for whom new land meant the establishment of families, the birth of traditions and the transplanting of racial cultures.

The western valley of the Mississippi invited with its fertility; it beckoned with its lush greenness. In the years which followed this tide of immigration the lands of the Louisiana Purchase produced, under the hands of these settlers, the limitless wealth which poured into the Standard Oil Company and Texaco, which fattened the grain markets on La Salle Street, the exchanges on Wall Street, and furnished motivation for the development of transportation that eventually linked, by common interests, two such widely diversified cities as New York and San Francisco. The settlement of this Mississippi Valley, then, was responsible for the establishment of unity and solidarity in the whole of these United States as we know them today.

In this westward surge of homesteaders who found the rich black loam of the prairies so much to their liking, we find a family which emigrated from Virginia to the Boon's Lick Country in Missouri. This family had a son who has brought a certain amount of fame to his adopted state. His name was George Caleb Bingham.

We are indebted to him for his lasting representations of the scenes which surrounded him, scenes which have kept alive for us today part of the seething, rugged and vigorous life which bequeathed to us the social and economic structure that is our own. Boats plying up and down these muddy rivers, teamsters, politicians, explorers, fur traders, illustrious names in the pages of American history, and nameless waifs who have comprised the backwash of our civilization—all are found on the canvases of this forthright, itinerant painter.

"The pageant which the painter (Bingham) saw began with the flood tide of immigration that bore his own family into the frontier region. He was able to observe at firsthand the hardy tribe of river boatmen, and later the stately procession of steamboats, which in turn gave way to the railways. He saw the passage of successive waves of immigrants bound for every Western state from Texas to Oregon.

"One of the first regions to feel the rush of immigration was the Boon's Lick Country in Missouri which was early reported to be prodigiously fertile. Settlers, among them the Bingham family, swarmed into this region from the East and South."[1]

Franklin, Missouri, was founded in 1812. By the year 1819, when the Bingham family settled there, it had become the most important center in the state west of the metropolis St. Louis.[2]

Washington Irving, traveling up the Missouri River in 1832, after the founding of Arrow Rock, wrote to his sister a brief but graphic picture of this country. He reveled in the magnificence of the wide prairies, which seemed to him more like cultivated gardens than the primitive rudeness of a wilderness. The fertility of the soil which produced deep and luxuriant forests surpassed anything that had yet come to his eye. The people, he wrote, with some amazement evident, were civil.[3]

It is not surprising, then, that within less than a decade a goodly number of migrants, seeking new homes in regions of abundance, should settle in this bountiful country to improve their new-found fortunes within the territory that was then Howard County. So it became necessary to establish a Land Office in Franklin in 1818, and there were made at this time the first land sales west of St. Louis. Interestingly enough, there is a commentary of sufficient length to give us a visual picture of the town of Franklin in 1817, just prior to its boom period. It then had about one

hundred and twenty crude log cabins one story high, a few frame structures of two stories and a few of brick, about a dozen stores, four taverns,
two smithies, two large team-mills, two "pool-halls," a log prison, post
office and court house.[4] But by 1819 many changes had been made; the
town was a hustling center of activity.

The first newspaper west of the Mississippi was published in Franklin
in 1819 and one year later a four-horse stage line ran transportation from
St. Louis to the then enterprising little city of Franklin.[5]

At a surprisingly early date the minds of the more intelligent and educated turned to the task of training their children; there was, no doubt,
a desire on the part of this group to incorporate into their new community
the opportunities for developing culture, for establishing traditions to
which they had been accustomed in their former homes. Contained in the
laws of Missouri, the first general assembly, first session, dated 1820, there
is recorded a notice that an academy be established in Franklin, to be
known as Franklin Academy.[6]

Among those who were listed as the trustees of this academy were
names prominent in the early history of the state. Most interesting to us
is the name of Nathaniel Hutchison, written second among the number
of trustees of this institution, for Hutchison was the father of the first
wife of George Caleb Bingham, Elizabeth Hutchison, whom he married
in 1836. This Hutchison, one of the incorporators of the town of New
Franklin and treasurer of the Masonic Lodge, was a man of outstanding
character and of some consequence.[7] The next signer was John J. Lowry,
a doctor of medicine and librarian of the Franklin Library Company.
Dr. Lowry rather sharply rebuked community book-borrowers in a
charmingly pointed notice in the local paper, revealing the fact that book-
borrowers are not changed in habit by changing location and, significant
to us, that the community, though pioneer, was by no means devoid of
those accessories which go to build up culture and refinement.[8]

Also among that number of far-visioned gentlemen who helped to
found this school on the very fringes of the western frontier were George
Tompkins and Jonathan S. Findlay. The former later became one of the
judges of the State Supreme Court, while Findlay, also a member of the

[3]

local Masonic Order, represented Howard County in 1820 at the Constitutional Convention.[9]

Other men of state-wide importance residing in Franklin at this time were Abiel Leonard, Nathaniel Patton, John Hardeman, and Dr. Hardage Lane, to mention only four of the most prominent of the community.

Leonard, a student of Dartmouth College from 1813 to 1815, was driven west by poverty. He began his career at Franklin as a school teacher, studied for the bar and was admitted in 1820. He eventually won wide recognition as a scholar and jurist, being elevated to the position of Justice of the Supreme Court of Missouri, and became a leader, if not the leader, of the Whig party of the state.[10] Nathaniel Patton, a man with great imagination, printed the *Missouri Intelligencer and Boon's Lick Advertiser* in Franklin in 1819. It was he who established the second printing press west of the Mississippi, the first west of St. Louis.[11] John Hardeman, a native of North Carolina, is known to all students of Missouriana as the man who developed the famous botanical gardens at Franklin. There is no question that he possessed wealth and culture; he claimed to be a graduate of Princeton University, though the University records do not verify this. He came to Missouri in 1819, the same year that Henry V. Bingham brought his family to Franklin from Virginia.[12]

Probably the first pioneer physician to settle in that community, and therefore in that section of the country, was Dr. Hardage Lane. His reputation for the hospitality he extended to the whole neighborhood, his interest in books and in art, is recorded in many state historical tracts.[13]

Josiah Gregg, author and artist, a talented and versatile man who wrote *The Commerce of the Prairies*, a rare story of the Santa Fe trade route, lived in this same Boon's Lick Country.[14] In this publication Gregg gives a picture of the importance of the town of Franklin, comparing it in importance with St. Louis. According to his account, Franklin seems to have been a most strategic commercial point, one which, until the Missouri River no longer carried the bulk of the transportation westward, was of significance difficult to appreciate today by those who are acquainted with the present routes and trade centers of Missouri.[15]

From the "Who's Who of the Franklin Union Lodge No. 7," Masonic

[4]

Order, there are listed names that reveal more of the civilized background of this remarkable boom-center.[16]

Henry V. Bingham, the father of George Caleb, is mentioned as one of the first county judges.[17] To have obtained a position of such importance, he must have been widely received in the community as a person worthy of respect, with a mind sufficiently trained to assume the responsibilities incumbent upon the office-holder. It would suggest, too, that Bingham senior was in a social position to hold daily contact with many, if not all, of the citizens introduced here.

A fellow member of the Masonic Order was one Hampton L. Boon, a sturdy contributor to communal life, educated for law, though primarily interested in the work of the church. He became Registrar of Lands at Franklin and, in 1842, Supreme Court Clerk at Jefferson City. While in residence there he edited the *Jefferson City Metropolitan*, a paper of considerable influence at the time.

The Masonic brotherhood had also initiated into its membership the Reverend Justinian Williams,[18] who, like so many of the earliest settlers, came from Virginia through Kentucky to Missouri. This man, a cabinet-maker and local preacher at Boonville in 1834, was the identical person to whom George Caleb Bingham was apprenticed as a boy of sixteen.[19]

Franklin was by no means a primitive, frontier settlement, with untutored yokels for its chief citizens, but rather a community whose leaders were men of deep culture. Men of remembered tradition and formal education formed its nucleus, from which grew and developed the civilization that later produced and fostered many of the illustrious names written in the history of the United States.

Now it would seem reasonable to suppose that the Bingham family had constant social intercourse with the accomplished and outstanding citizens of this community. Mary Amend Bingham,[20] an intelligent, educated woman, undoubtedly was acclaimed by her fellow citizens; a woman who, in 1823, had the temper and quality to face the world with her fatherless children and win from it a livelihood.[21] Courageously she directed their minds to higher growth as she attempted to mold their futures.

It was in this environment, surrounded by virile, adventuresome, educated, and high-minded folk, that George Caleb Bingham grew to manhood. It would seem logically false to assume that the growth and development of the artist was a miraculous and mysterious appearance of genius strange to a wild and uncultured settlement.

Naturally there has been much speculation relating to the genius of George Caleb Bingham, "the Missouri artist." How, some ask, could such creative ability be developed in "squalid, straggling towns in the Middle West," just as they ask this identical question about his contemporary fellow Missourian, Samuel Clemens.[22] And so to answer this question there has been a growing tendency on the part of critics since the "Bingham revival," beginning approximately in 1934,[23] to want to attribute to Bingham's training some potent extra-western influence, preferably in the person of some great European-trained painter. As indicated in a later chapter, it would seem doubtful, if not impossible, that Bingham as a boy knew the painter Harding personally.[24] It is more logical and natural to assume that he had frequent contact, perhaps, with various itinerant painters who passed through Franklin, Arrow Rock and Boonville.[25] In his father's tavern at Franklin on the highway of transcontinental communication, Bingham, as a boy, may have held the reins for many an eastern traveler stopping overnight in this center.

The Missouri River, on or near which Bingham spent these early years, carried large transportation, and George conceivably could have stood on dock and wharf to recognize many a face which was well known across the continent. And the educated and imaginative pioneer, like those described, brought culture of a high type to the Missouri town. Josiah Gregg, for instance, himself an artist, would probably mean more to the boy's everyday growth by constant contact than the hurried visit of a Chester Harding. "His boyhood was spent upon the banks of the Missouri; and never, since he reached the stature of manhood, has he been East of the Mississippi. Except those of his own execution, he never saw a portrait painted in his life."[26]

" 'All that goes to make the me in me was in a Missourian village on the other side of the globe,' Mark Twain wrote in India, looking back through the vista of three score years."[27] George Caleb Bingham might have written this same sentiment from Düsseldorf, for he belonged in the West, both as painter and politician, and he seems always to have been aware of that. Because he was so authentically of Franklin and Boonville and Arrow Rock, he was, like Mark Twain, "authentically of Missouri and authentically of America—for Missouri lies at the cross-roads of the nation." [28]

The Heritage

WHAT little is known about the ancestors of George Caleb Bingham was written hurriedly by the artist in a brief sketch evidently intended to preface an autobiography which he began but, unfortunately, never completed. Because he wrote in a lucid and pleasing style, this self-portrait would have been engrossing history; and because fame is searching him out, it could have been an invaluable document to add to America's swelling volumes commemorating the great of our brief but increasingly important past.

"I have no knowledge of my ancestry beyond my maternal and paternal grandfathers. The former was born of German parentage near the city of Little York in the state of Pennsylvania. His name was Matthias Amend. He was by trade a millwright and a most excellent workman in his line. Before the close of the last century he migrated to the valley of Virginia and settled at the place on which is the celebrated cavern known as Wier's Cave. Through his grounds flowed the beautiful little South River, which forms one of the three branches of the Shenandoah that intersect each other near the village of Port Republic. Upon this never-failing stream he erected a sawmill and gristmill which furnished lumber and breadstuff to the community for miles around. Its revolving wheels were the earliest wonder upon which my eyes opened, and as an evidence of the skill with which they were constructed, they are yet in motion after a lapse of more than three score years. But two children were born to my Grandfather Amend, a son and a daughter. The former died in early childhood. The death of the mother soon followed, and the daughter, Mary, was the only remaining solace to the bereaved millwright. Upon her were quite naturally centered all his hopes and affections. Having been the child of poverty himself and, consequently, favored with none of the advantages of education, his experience of the evils of such a deprivation impelled him to obtain for his daughter such means of instruction as the country then afforded. The nearest school was six miles from his residence. This Mary attended from the house of a kinsman near-by, to which she went every Monday morning, never failing to return to her father on the succeeding Saturday, in the evening of which and the Sunday following she would impart to him the lessons she had received during the week.

"Thus father and child were educated together, the child obtaining a good English education, and the father learning to read and write and to cast up accounts.

"My grandfather, George Bingham, was born and raised in some of the New England states, from which at about the close of the Revolution he migrated to Virginia and settled on the east side of the Blue Ridge, about eighteen miles west of Charlottesville, the home of Jefferson and the seat of the Virginia University.

"He was what is termed a local Methodist preacher and as such ministered to a congregation in a meeting-house erected for their accommodation upon his plantation. He cultivated tobacco and grain by the aid of a number of slaves, to whom he was exceedingly kind and indulgent, never using the lash or allowing it to be used upon his place.

"I remember him well as a tall and white-haired old gentleman, overflowing with the milk of human kindness. He had three sons and four daughters who reached the age of maturity. My father, Henry V. Bingham, was the oldest son and the oldest child. He was blessed with a good constitution, and leading from early boyhood an active life, he presented in his person at the time of my remembrance a fine specimen of vigorous manhood, measuring six feet in height and weighing over a hundred and eighty pounds. His education was only such as could be acquired in the common field schools of the time, but he was a constant reader, and his mind became stored with a good amount of historical and political information.

"After reaching his twenty-first year he had the charge of his father's plantation and conducted its affairs with energy and industry, laboring in the fields with the slaves and taking the annual crop of tobacco to market in Richmond.

"The present era of railroads and rapid transportation furnishes a striking contrast to the roads and locomotive powers which then furnished the Virginian with the only means of reaching a market with a staple upon which he predicated his hope of future wealth. Not even the common wagon was used. Each hogshead of tobacco was strongly hooped from end to end, the heads were made of thick and substantial material, and in the center of each was inserted a strong hickory pin to which a pair of shafts were attached, and by which a single horse could roll a hogshead of tobacco from the shed in which it was prepared from fifty to a hundred miles, as the distance might be, to the market which furnished a purchaser.

"This was generally done at a season of the year when the roads were dry, and when the labor both of horses and men could be best spared from the fields. At such times the roads to Richmond would be filled for miles at a stretch with 'tobacco rollers' who enlivened the hours with singing songs and cracking their jokes. Some of the latter were occasionally of a practical nature and calculated to test the temper of their unfortunate subjects.

"Taking his provisions and blankets with him, each roller would encamp, and frequently alone, wherever he might be at the approach of night, and in the event of a cloudy morning it not infrequently happened that a roller, after attaching his horse and traveling several miles, would be astonished by meeting a roller traveling exactly the opposite of the course which appeared to him to be the way to Richmond. Questions and answers would be immediately exchanged which would make it clear to his mind that the shafts of his hogshead, which were toward Richmond when he laid down, had been reversed by some wicked rival while he was asleep, and that deceived thereby he was wending his way homeward instead of lessening his distance to Richmond. Should he meet in Richmond the wag who thus tricked him, a fight might ensue, or a jolly laugh and a drink all around, as the humor of the parties might happen to be.

"In consequence of the entire failure of the mill streams on the east side of the Blue Ridge during a period of drouth, it became necessary for my father to take a load of grain 'over the mountain' to my Grandfather

Amend's mill on the South River. While there he became acquainted, as a matter of course, with my mother, Mary Amend, fell in love with her, and in due time offered himself in marriage and was accepted.

"As my mother, Mary, was the only treasure which my Grandfather Amend valued, in giving her away, he also surrendered to my father his entire earthly possessions, stipulating only that he should have a home with his daughter during the period of his natural life.[1]

"As soon, therefore, as the wedding was consummated, my father became the proprietor of the lands including the mill and Wier's Cave, so called in honor of its discoverer, a little Dutchman named Barnett Wier, who was in the habit of roaming among the hills and forests with his dog and gun." [2]

From the facts contained in Bingham's account, plus the information obtained from Virginia records, then, it would seem that both Henry Vest Bingham [3] and Mary Amend came from substantial families. Unquestionably, they were reared to respect education and did what they could to improve their minds by attending the schools that were nearby and reading those books to which they had access. "Both were of honorable character, and the mother, particularly, was very intelligent." [4]

In 1819 Henry Vest Bingham was forced to surrender the vast holdings deeded to him by his father-in-law and moved, with his family, to Missouri, where he hoped to regain his wealth in that fertile territory then known as the Boon's Lick Country.

The Early Life

GEORGE CALEB BINGHAM was born on a plantation of one thousand one hundred and eighty acres on the South River in Augusta County, Virginia, March 20, 1811. Very little is known concerning his early boyhood years in Virginia. However, from an early biographical sketch [1] we read that at an early age he was interested in drawing, and that his father, too, sometimes took the pencil to represent any object matter which caught his fancy. This account tells of what supposedly was the boy's initial attempt at drawing. We may imagine that George amused himself by drawing and tried to represent the interesting objects about him. He continued to practice with unfailing interest; and when he was twelve he had developed the ability to copy with commendable faithfulness various drawings and engravings to which he gained access in the home or which might have been given him by interested friends. [2]

It is possible that many engravings of the work of the Renaissance masters fell into the hands of the boy, for there is no doubt that in later years his composition of many pictures is reminiscent of such masters as, for example, Poussin and Canaletto. Arthur Pope ventures: "Bingham must have gotten his lessons in composition from engravings after Renaissance-Baroque masters, for there is constant use of pictorial forms derived from sixteenth and seventeenth century painting." [3] In a home where a library was considered of some importance, [4] Bingham must have read about and examined various drawings and engravings upon which he happened to chance. In his study of them he was no doubt encouraged by his family.

In 1819, because of financial reverses in Virginia, his father having lost through a security debt most of the money left him by his father-in-law, [5] the family was attracted by the lure of free lands and rich soil and moved to Missouri. Had Henry V. Bingham lived more than the four years that he spent in Howard County, he probably could have re-established the family fortunes. "Rich clay, loam soil of that territory proved profitable for tobacco raising." [6] With a partner Bingham erected a tobacco factory in Franklin,[7] purchased a farm of one hundred and sixty acres in Arrow Rock Township, and became owner of a tavern at Franklin.[8]

During this period young George was afforded those advantages which the home and community offered, while he continued to play, to study and to draw. There is an account by Fern Helen Rusk in her *George Caleb Bingham, the Missouri Artist* concerning the visit of Chester Harding to Boon's Lick in 1820 to paint the portrait of Daniel Boone. She speculates that George, a lad of nine years, might have watched part of the process of the execution of this painting. This seems improbable because the old frontiersman, according to a recognized authority, Hazel A. Spraker, did not live at Boon's Lick but at the home of his son-in-law, Mr. Flanders Callaway, near the village of Marthasville in Warren County.[9] This village, according to Mr. Roy King of the Missouri Historical Society, was some one hundred miles from Franklin and Boon's Lick, and therefore the probability that George witnessed the actual painting of the picture seems minute.[10]

Although this probability discounts the idea that Harding was the single potent inspiration of the boy, considerable influence may have been exerted by other itinerant artists, as well as by members of the community who were interested in pictures.

At the age of twelve, however, George's boyhood activities abruptly ceased with the assumption of grown-up responsibilities. On December 26, 1823, Mrs. Bingham was a widowed mother with six children to support. Most probably she did not leave their old home immediately, but she opened her school for girls in Franklin shortly after the death of her husband. It is recorded that "she had a good, even if small, library of English literature which she had saved and from which George obtained his foundation for the excellent command of English which he evinced in later life." [11]

Because of unfortunate mismanagement the extensive properties of the Bingham family dwindled until finally they were left with the one-hundred-and-sixty-acre farm near Arrow Rock. There is a report [12] in the

[13]

Masonic records of Franklin that in the early part of 1827 Mrs. Bingham sought aid of the fellow members of the deceased husband's Lodge and that they secured for her the farm near Arrow Rock, to which she soon afterward moved her family.[13]

C. B. Rollins states in his *Recollections of George Caleb Bingham* that, when a lad of sixteen, George was apprenticed to a cabinetmaker in Boonville.[14] In the *History of Saline County* there is information which leads to an interesting speculation concerning this period of his life. "Jesse Green, a cabinet maker during the week, and a Methodist minister on Sundays, was a pioneer preacher who lived near Arrow Rock. In his shop Geo. C. Bingham, Missouri's greatest artist and one of her best sons, first worked and here sketched his first pictures with chalk, before he went to Boonville." [15] It seems probable, then, that George went with the family to Arrow Rock, was apprenticed to Green for a short time, and upon Green's transfer to the Shawnee District, went to Boonville to the shop of Green's fellow associate in trade and in the Methodist Church, Justinian Williams.[16]

There he obtained instruction in religion and was given further opportunity to continue his reading. At least we know that George was interested at various times in becoming either a lawyer or a minister.[17] The knowledge of the Bible as well as his study of literature stood him in good stead many times in later life.[18] "He frequently preached at the camp meetings common in those days. I have heard him tell the story that on one occasion after he had finished the sermon, one of his auditors came forward and tendered him a silver dollar, saying his sermon was well worth the money," [19] Mr. Rollins reports.

About this time, also, he studied law for a few months with Washington Adams, later Judge of the Supreme Court of the State, "but the siren call of Bingham's first love, Art, was louder than that of the law, the ministry or the square and chisel, and at the age of nineteen or twenty he was painting portraits at twenty dollars each, frames included." [20]

When Bingham was about nineteen years of age he attempted a trip to St. Louis, intending to study there. "But sometime before he reached his destination he was attacked by measles and lay in an old log cabin, completely deserted, save for a young doctor and an old negress, who cared for him. The negress could not be induced to go near the sufferer, but she poked food and drink through a crack into the cabin, and the doctor nursed Bingham carefully until he was strong enough to care for himself. Completely shattered in health, it was impossible for him to complete his journey; so he returned to his home in Saline County." [21] This seems to be corroborated by the following account by C. B. Rollins: "When Bingham was about nineteen years old he had a severe attack of measles which left him bald and ever since he had worn a wig." [22]

Bingham, after his discouraging illness and upon his recuperation in his home at Arrow Rock, probably returned to Franklin; it was here that he presumably did his first work as a professional painter, for we learn from a letter published in the *Missouri Statesman* that a studio "was gratuitously placed at his disposal." [23] From a brief account of the artist's life published in the *Columbia Statesman*, August 31, 1849, we note that he located at Arrow Rock and there "resumed the occasional use of the lead pencil" and made sketches of four young men of his acquaintance who "proposed to sit to him for their portraits, taking upon themselves the risk of his success. He accepted the proposition, and with such colors as a house-painter's shop could supply, and a half-dozen stumps of brushes left by a transient artist in a neighboring town, he commenced his career as a portrait painter. By becoming to some extent an itinerant, and painting upon moderate terms, he found himself full of business, and though in total darkness in regard to color, his drawing generally gave so strong a likeness that many of his unsophisticated patrons looked upon his productions as the perfection of the 'divine art.' He astonished them, too, by his facility of execution, frequently commencing and finishing a portrait in the same day. It is said that he painted, in this manner, twenty-five in the course of thirty days." [24] Though at first thought the two articles just quoted seem to conflict, it is perfectly conceivable that during these years Bingham developed his first technical abilities, traveling as much as possible, yet confining himself mostly to the two centers, Franklin and Arrow Rock. One of his constant companions at this time was H. H. Hutchison, younger brother of Bingham's future wife, Elizabeth. Bingham used to pay young Hutchison small amounts of money to "sit still for half an hour while he made fancy sketches." [25] From every indication it seems that Bingham's energies were turned constantly to the business of making himself master of the rudiments of his profession.

The Early Work

By 1834, when the young portrait painter came to Columbia, taking a studio on Guitar Street, he had quite fully mastered the essential techniques of the painter. That he was received there with enthusiasm can be seen from a newly discovered article printed in the Columbia paper, the *Missouri Intelligencer*, March 14, 1835.[1] This interesting commentary, the earliest of any importance yet found, is of sufficient significance to warrant its being placed verbatim into our account.

"The Fine Arts—We cannot refrain from expressing our delight, occasioned by a visit, a few mornings since, to the portrait-room of Mr. Bingham, upon Guitar street. Upon entering, our sensations partook more of the nature of surprise, than of any other emotion. A collection of well finished portraits—each affording full evidence of a cultivated mimetic skill, and of an undoubted high creative genius—is a circumstance, that deserves a place as an important era, in the history of Trans-Mississippian progress, towards a state of intellectual and social refinement. We attach no more importance to this matter than it really deserves. The estimation in which painting has been held, and the patronage which has been bestowed on those excellent in the profession, will be found, in looking at all past time, to have been exalted and liberal, in proportion as the country or age was marked by the spirit of improvement or animated by the busy foot-steps of advancement, in the spread and culture of all the higher enjoyments and distinguishing excellencies of life and manners.

"These remarks are made, not with a view of complimenting our own village,—because here alone of all the upper towns, which he visited, was any thing like a deserving patronage extended the young Boon's Lick artist—but for the purpose of giving just credit, to the incipient character of society, in one of the youngest sisters of the Union.

"Of Mr. Bingham himself, we would say a word. As a painter, whatever he is, he is by means of his own unassisted application, and untutored study. His boyhood was spent upon the banks of the Missouri; and never, since he reached the stature of manhood, has he been East of the Mississippi. Except those of his own execution, he never saw a portrait painted in his life. Aware of these facts, there is no one who can enter his room, without being struck with more than admiration, with the many evidences of a deep, native originality, which surround his portraits. We are unacquainted, save to a degree, with the works of Eastern artists, but it is tho't that the portraits of Mr. Bingham might be placed along side the finest specimens of Harding, Catlin, and Duett, and receive honor from the comparison. If we might venture a criticism upon Mr. Bingham, as an artist, we should say, that of the three Italian schools, his style combines more of the excellencies of the Leontine and Venetian, than of the Lombard. His skill is more fortunately displayed in the design, delineation, and coloring, than in the most effective use of, as it is technically termed, *chiaro-scure.*—We think, likewise, that the pencil of our artist might be permitted, occasionally, a stroke or two more of flattery, with advantage. In some instances too faithful a copy of features is unfavorable to effect. But we do not pretend to be a connoisseur in the art pictorial, and possibly may be mistaken in our opinions.

"Mr. B., we understand, is now paying a visit to St. Louis, where no doubt his merits will meet with a proper appreciation. Those, at St. Louis, of the friends of the presiding officer of the 1st Judicial district, can see a very accurate and striking likeness, by calling at the room of Mr. Bingham; and will also have an opportunity of judging for themselves concerning the talents and genius of this self-taught artist.

"St. Louis must continue, for a long time, the principal nursery of the fine arts, in 'the far west'; and, it is hoped, that as the Metropolis of Missouri, she will take an especial pride in fostering the native genius of the State. If the West will but extend a cherishing patronage, she can rear up, from the number of her youth, sons of genius, that, like the trees of her own deep forests, will attain the largest and the stateliest growth. If the young artist, who has called forth these remarks, possesses the talents which we conceive, let them be excited and drawn out by liberality of encouragement at home, and ere long, the country shall see with delight, and hear with pleasure, the productions and the praises,—to borrow a title of Rubens—of a Western 'meteor of the art.'"

This article, with its charmingly archaic style of writing and its evident local pride, was without question written by one who had some well-founded knowledge of the history of the fine arts. We would be ungrateful not to express our appreciation to this early enthusiast of painting for the delightfully phrased account which reveals a few of Bingham's artistic

GEORGE CALEB BINGHAM
SELF-PORTRAIT

Plate I
No. 2

JAMES S. ROLLINS

Plate I
No. 1

accomplishments in this phase of his growth.

During this stay in Columbia, Bingham obtained commissions from some of the most prominent residents of that town, among whom can be listed Major James S. Rollins (Pl. I, No. 1), Colonel Caleb S. Stone, Judge Warren Woodson, and the Honorable Josiah Wilson. These portraits are of great interest and significance to those interested in the study of the artist's artistic development because they are the first to represent that crystalline clarity of draughtsmanship, precise definition of planes, and unfailing analysis of the personality of the sitter which make the superior works of Bingham such a revelation of his stature as an artist.

Mr. C. B. Rollins tells an anecdote concerning the portraits of Rollins, Woodson, and Wilson. These three portraits, completed nearly simultaneously, were among that "collection of well finished portraits—each affording full evidence of a cultivated mimetic skill, and of an undoubted high creative genius." The three gentlemen, arriving together to collect their respective portraits, were struck by the evident similarity of the technical handling, the posture, and the light source in each of the pictures. They, to the amusement of the painter, made a pretense of not being able to distinguish one portrait from another. So the artist asked each to choose any one of them for his own. "In reality, the pictures do resemble each other somewhat. In the first place, all three of the young men had black hair and ruddy complexions and wore the stiff-bosom shirt, the broad revers and the inevitable high stock. Then, the manner of treatment of the three is the same. All are placed in the same lighting, all present a left three-quarters view of the face and bust and, evidently, all have been told to look at the same spot while their pictures were being made." [2]

An examination of the portrait of the young Columbia lawyer, James S. Rollins [3] (Plate I, No. 1), shows the subject to be a strikingly handsome man of about twenty-two,[4] with a face of strength and intelligence, giving promise of that fine sense of proportion which eventually made him one of the political leaders of the state, and revealing that refinement which led him to become, through the years in which he lived in Columbia, a patron of the arts and of learning.[5]

During the spring of 1834, after young Rollins had completed his studies for the bar and had settled in an office on the same street where Bingham had his studio,[6] there was begun a friendship which spanned, unbroken, a period of forty-five years, a friendship which was characterized by selfless mutual giving and harmonious understanding.

To obtain an authentic picture of George Caleb Bingham, his physical appearance, his personality and character; to make vivid the person, with his temperament and his idiosyncrasies we must now turn to the Rollins family, of Columbia, Missouri, for "he (Bingham) found a patron on the frontier, a whole family of patrons in the Rollins clan of Columbia, Missouri. They were a distinguished lot and one of their clan loyalties that endured through two generations was to Bingham." [7]

During an era of nearly half a century, approximately a thousand letters must have passed between Rollins and Bingham.[8] Of these, one hundred and thirty-five, written by Bingham to Rollins, were preserved by the recipient. For many years these valuable letters were not to be located. Finally, however, Mr. C. B. Rollins found them lying, undamaged by time, in a barrel in the basement of the old Rollins home in Columbia, Missouri. He and Mr. Floyd Shoemaker, secretary of the State Historical Society of Missouri, read them carefully and decided to place them in the files of the Society's Manuscript Room, housed in the library building of the University of Missouri.[9]

From the spirit of the correspondence between these two men we have another heart-warming example of high-minded aspiration and mutual trust incorporated in a manly feeling of friendship, which has been likened to that of David and Jonathan.[10] It is from these letters that we reconstruct much of what was personal in the life of the artist and receive further new light on his artistic and political career. Though the letters are not always in close sequence, "they give the thread and tenor of his life and reveal him somewhat as he appeared to those who knew him best." [11] They "reveal a most tender attachment, a confidence utterly unreserved, and a sense of irremovable obligation that is never once felt as a burden." [12] The letters, supported by other manuscripts of speeches and articles on varied subject matter, from religion to politics, serve further to portray the man, his power to express himself boldly, subtly, and adequately in the medium of words as well as pigment. These letters are invaluable in the reconstruction of the intimate picture of Bingham. In them the artist unconsciously reveals his breadth of interest; his unlimited activism; his deeply religious mind and puritan Christian character; his strength of will and unbending loyalty to his convictions; his loving kindness to his family and friends.

As invaluable, too, are the recollections of the man who is today the only remaining link in that long chain of friendship—the Honorable C. B. Rollins, native Missourian, a careful student of history, and a patron of education. Mr. Rollins is the son of Major James S. Rollins, and in his eighty-sixth year recalls with the exactness of a trained memory his personal relationship with the artist. His reminiscences are the most important and most accurate connection between our day and the later life of Bingham.

Thus, in searching these sources as well as a few newly discovered articles in newspapers contemporary with the artist,[13] we mold a life-size figure of the man. And in the modeling we see in image before us a figure impressive with vitality, stimulating with rich living, capacious in understanding, challenging in courage, and noble with generosity.[14]

The Adventure

It is difficult to say exactly when Bingham fulfilled his early desire to visit St. Louis. From the early newspaper account [1] we learned that "Mr. B., we understand, is now paying a visit to St. Louis," while from a record in the *Jeffersonian Republican*, January 2, 1836, there is an excerpt from the *St. Louis Bulletin* which states: "He (Bingham) came to St. Louis a few weeks since, warm with enthusiasm, and full of the hope, that with the proper instruction and attention, he could distinguish himself in his profession." Making allowance for the inaccuracy of newspaper reporters, we can only arrive at the general conclusion that he did "set up his stand" as portrait painter in the metropolis sometime in the year 1835.

It is thought by some that Bingham studied in St. Louis, that perhaps at this time he received instruction from Chester Harding.[2] At any rate, he probably met and associated with cultivated and influential families of that city. He "found a welcome reception among our citizens" and he enjoyed a profitable business. This is pleasantly recorded in the *Jeffersonian Republican*, January 2, 1836:

"The Fine Arts.—We were much pleased with a visit a day or two since to the Painting Room of Mr. Bingham, on Market-street, where we found some as good portraits of a few of our well known citizens as we could expect to see from the pencil of any artist, as young in the profession as Mr. B.

"Mr. Bingham, though not a native of the State of Missouri, has been a resident of Cooper county from infancy. His first efforts in portrait painting were made about [line here is unreadable] and the success he there met with, induced him to try his fortunes where he could find a wide field for enterprise and better school for instruction. He came to St. Louis a few weeks since, warm with enthusiasm, and full of the hope, that with proper instruction and attention, he could distinguish himself in his profession. He has, we are happy to say, found a welcome reception among our citizens, his patronage has been as extensive as he could have wished, and we have

[22]

but little doubt that if he devotes that time and attention to the profession he has undertaken, which it requires, he will in the event meet the warmest anticipations of his friends. His success in portrait painting is all the result of perseverance and his own genius, no master's hand directed his pencil, no wise head pointed out his faults—he alone designed and executed. His portraits are invariably good, yet there is a want of skill in coloring evinced, which does not disclose a want of genius, but of instruction. His portrait of Fanny Kemble from an engraving in 'The Gift,' is we consider, one of his best efforts. The delicate and beautifully blended tints of the cheek are inferior to but few of the best paintings of the day, and we have no doubt, that with the patronage on the part of our citizens, a due regard to his profession, Mr. B. will at no remote time, become an ornament to his profession, and an honor to Missouri."

In a letter written from St. Louis to his fiancée, Miss Elizabeth Hutchison of Boonville, he states his intention "to struggle for a while alone" with the hope that he might win security for himself, care for his mother, "and be even with the world." [3] This is a characteristic instance of his strength of will, his long-sightedness and devotion to a sense of duty which later in life motivated him to take undaunted his stand on questions of state-wide, even national, importance. In this letter he writes further of his profession and of his determination to use every exertion to distinguish himself as a painter.[4] The ambitious determination, apparently always possessing him, driving his restive mind, was never more in evidence than now, when, confronted with the handicap of poverty and strange to the ways of the metropolis, he laid the foundation stones of his career.[5]

His self-portrait, 1835 (Pl. I, No. 2), shows more subtly and deeply the character as well as the artistic ability of this young man of twenty-four than can be expressed in words. This portrait, now excellently restored under the supervision of Meyric R. Rogers, formerly director of the St. Louis City Museum where it now hangs, shows a strong, even stubborn face, deep-set, dark eyes piercing out from under heavy, well-shaped eyebrows and communicating to the observer the sharply analytical intelligence he possessed. A well-modeled, straight and strong nose is set out in bold relief against rather high-set cheek bones and full cheeks. The mouth discloses a ghost of a suggestion of humor with its lightly upturned ends, remarks also in the shape of the lower lip of a proud and even willful spirit. The chin, slightly cleft, is comfortably square and rugged, and its strength counterbalances the wide space of slightly jutting forehead. The drawing of the hair line reveals perfectly, without apology or attempt at deceit, the wig which so many times was the cause of startling incident and embarrassed amusement.

It has been held that, when the painting is compared with a photograph of Bingham in the possession of Mr. C. B. Rollins, it seems to be a compensation for Bingham's unquestioned egotism, for, some say, the painting makes him appear really more handsome than he was at the time. An examination of the photograph, however, leads the writer to question this observation. Moreover, Bingham carried a reputation for painting portraits realistically, even at that early date, for we read in a criticism written on March 14, 1835, that he was sometimes too faithful a draughtsman to please the conceit of the sitter.[6]

Upon his return from St. Louis in 1836, Bingham married Miss Hutchison. This marriage took place in April, according to his own letter. From this time the young couple lived with Bingham's mother at Arrow Rock in a house reputedly built by Bingham's own hands. We may safely assume that by this time Bingham had established a reputation for industry and responsibility.

His wife's family was prominent in Franklin.[7] Her father was a member of the board of trustees of Franklin Academy, and she herself was many times referred to as a "very charming and beautiful, amiable and intelligent" girl of seventeen years. She bore him three children during the following twelve years.

It is quite definite that Bingham and his young bride, after spending perhaps the greater part of the summer and fall at Arrow Rock, left for St. Louis, to continue to Natchez after a brief meeting with the artist's friend Rollins. The trip was designed to serve a twofold purpose: to recuperate Bingham's health and to paint some of the distinguished citizens of Mississippi.[8] At least we know that Bingham received sufficient commissions at sums adequate to support him and his wife. At Vicksburg, where he spent a brief period, he painted the portrait of Sergeant S. Prentiss. He was greatly impressed with the brilliant orator from New England.[9]

Just before Bingham's return to Columbia, he wrote his first known letter to James S. Rollins—a letter of sufficient importance to warrant its inclusion in this biography. At this time Bingham had passed through the initial stages of development in his work and had gained some measure of recognition. In this letter he expresses that spirit of unconquerable will to do which was so typical of him.

"Natchez, May 6, 1837

"My dear Sir,

"I at last take upon myself the task of writing a letter. It, however, becomes a pleasant one, when performed in addressing an old and valued friend. You recollect when we met last winter in St. Louis, it was then my intention to have returned immediately to Boonville, preparatory for a trip to the east, but bad roads and broken stages rendered it impossible, and two or three days after you left, myself and wife also departed for the South. We overtook your boat, the Vandalia, at Vicksburg, and as we landed for a few minutes I went on board of her, anticipating the pleasure of seeing you, but tho 'the nest was there and still warm, the bird had flown;' you had just walked up into the city and I was disappointed. That night at 11 o'clock we arrived at Natchez, and after remaining two weeks, I succeeded in getting a room and commenced business. I have been regularly employed during the winter, at from $40 to $60 per portrait, and flattered myself that I was doing well, notwithstanding the exorbitant price of living in this country.

"But circumstances which now exist here, must deprive me of the benefit of my earnings for at least 6 or 8 months. The Agricultural and Planters Banks of this city, both stopped payment on the 2nd inst. and their notes to those who are compelled to leave here are almost valueless. The immediate cause of failure of the Agricultural Bank, was a demand from the Treasury of the U. S. for one hundred and twenty thousand dollars, she being one of the pet banks. As the sum was rather larger than could be spared conveniently, it was deemed most prudent not to pay it. The Planters Bank immediately followed suit.

"The notes of these banks constituted the principal currency of the country, and the state of affairs which their failure has produced is truly alarming. It is apprehended that almost every institution of the kind in the state will immediately suspend specie payments. It is useless to attempt to give an

[25]

adequate idea of the pressure for money that prevails throughout the South. The most literal statement of facts must appear to those who are at a distance, as the ebulition of an overheated imagination. A week or two since, in another quarter of this State, a gentleman having in his possession a few one-hundred-dollar U. S. notes was induced to put them up to the highest bidder, at a few months' credit, the purchaser giving bond and ample security. They sold for two hundred and fifty dollars apiece.

"Almost every countenance is shrouded in gloom in anticipation of the distress which must be produced this summer.

"All this is attributed to the interference of the government with the established currency of the country, and to the Treasury Circular.

"I expect to leave this place in a few days for Missouri and will perhaps spend the best part of the summer there. I will try and visit Columbia, and if you could procure me subscribers for a dozen portraits at $25 I should be glad to remain with you six or eight weeks previous to making a trip eastward. I cannot foresee where my destiny will lead me, it may become my interest to settle in some one of the eastern cities. The greater facilities afforded there, for improvement in my profession, would be the principal inducement. There is no honorable sacrifice which I would not make to attain eminence in the art to which I have devoted myself. I am aware of the difficulties in my way, and am cheered by the thought that they are no greater than those which impeded the course of Harding and Sully and many others. It is by combatting that we can overcome them, and by determined perseverance I expect to be successful.

"Are you yet in the state of single blessedness? If so, I trust for your own credit that it will not long be the case. Do get a wife, and get children, and get me to paint you a family group.

". . . I trust it will not be long before I see you all once more. I will be in Boonville in three weeks from this date, and you must write to me there.
"Yours.   G. C. Bingham.
"J. S. Rollins, Esqr."

Upon Bingham's arrival in Columbia, Rollins evidently had procured enough subscribers for portraits so that Bingham could earn the money he needed for his contemplated trip to the East. Some of the more prominent Columbia residents who sat for him were Doctor Anthony W. Rollins, Mrs. Anthony W. Rollins, Mr. David Steel Lamme, Mrs. David Steel Lamme and son,[10] the Honorable Roger North Todd, General Richard

DR. OSCAR F. POTTER

PLATE II
NO. 2

MRS. ANTHONY ROLLINS

PLATE II
NO. 1

Gentry, Judge Henry Lewis, Mrs. Elizabeth Lewis, Major James S. Rollins, Mrs. James S. Rollins, and President Thomas Miller of Columbia College.

The portrait of Mrs. Anthony Rollins (Plate II, No. 1) has much of that severity and penetration which is marked in the *Self Portrait*, but it possesses "more charm and beauty of paint quality. The goffered cap and the other simple costume accessories are rendered with painter-like skill, and used with reserve but considerable decorative effect. When viewed apart from the sentimental and impressionist preoccupations of the last century these first efforts of Bingham are full of significance for unusual native gifts are apparent which in a more favorable age and environment might well have borne fruit of the greatest rarity." [11]

The Eastern Influence

IN THE fall of 1837 Bingham left Columbia for Philadelphia where he studied in the Academy of Fine Arts for three months.[1] "Here he must have come into contact with the work of artists of the Revolutionary period of American art, most important among them Gilbert Stuart, the great portrait painter, who had received his training in England in the time of the notable English portrait painters, Sir Joshua Reynolds and Thomas Gainsborough. A number of years later Bingham made copies of Stuart's Athenaeum portraits of George and Martha Washington. Among contemporaries whose work he must have seen in Philadelphia are Thomas Sully, portrait painter, and John Neagle, whose portrait—almost genre—of Pat Lyons painted in 1826 excited so much interest on account of its truthful representation of the sturdy character of the blacksmith. Above all, Bingham now had an opportunity of seeing genre paintings, the branch of art which interested him most. He, like many another in his day, gave a great deal of time to portraiture, though considering it a comparatively low form of art, because it was the surest and quickest source of income. It was to literary subjects that he aspired, to pictures that tell a story. So he must have been interested in the work of Inman and other genre painters who were working in Philadelphia at the time. No doubt he began making sketches of genre scenes himself, though we have no definite knowledge of any of his work in that line until several years later." [2]

It is perhaps unfortunate that Bingham spent these few months in Philadelphia when, so inexperienced, he was impressionable to an extent not beneficial to his subsequent work in portraiture. "The dexterity of Stuart and the suave sentimentality of Sully were allures too glamorous for the young artist to entirely resist." [3] It can be only a matter of speculation as to the trend that Bingham's mind and painting technique might have taken had it not been for some of the ideas which, poorly digested, standardized rather than heightened the arresting individuality shown in his early painting manner.

It is known, too, that in 1838 he spent some time in New York City, where he probably again studied. In the latter part of the year "he returned to his home at Arrow Rock and continued to practice his profession, devoting himself principally to portraiture. He painted a great number of portraits of men and women of Saline, Cooper, Howard, Boone, and other counties. Photography was not yet known. The portrait was the only method by which our fathers could transmit their likenesses to future generations. The desire not to be entirely forgotten was as strong then as now and prompted many to have their features committed to canvas. Back in those days, not to have a Bingham portrait on the wall of the parlor was as rare as not to have a Bible on the center table." [4]

Because of his new found interest in genre, it may be that even at this early date he began to sketch his impressions of the panorama of the vigorous, hardy life in the country and along the river.

The Political Influence

SOMETIME in the spring of 1840, Bingham became involved actively in the presidential campaign, which created a great stir throughout the state. The big Whig convention was to be held at Rocheport in June.[1] "Great mass meetings, to which people came from many miles, were held. They often lasted for several days. Distinguished speakers used all the oratory they could muster, and banners, music and hard cider helped to keep the enthusiasm that prevailed."[2] All the counties neighboring Rocheport were vying with one another to develop the most unique and striking banners to swing popular sentiment for "Old Tippecanoe and Tyler too." Naturally, Bingham was approached with many an offer to design and paint a banner appropriate to the occasion.

Thomas Miller, then president of Columbia College, wrote to the artist in May, 1840, to request that Bingham paint some posters for Boone County. That he declined the offer is quite typical of Bingham and bespeaks the fact that he held his work up to the light of his high standards, even though it might be merely a banner used temporarily. Already busy with a similar work for Saline County, he replied to Miller that the design must be worthy of the occasion.[3] Surely it must be attributed to this quality of conscientiousness in him that he already, as a young man, had mastered that subtlety and strength of draughtsmanship which causes competent critics of our day to recall the French seventeenth century [4] and to see "shades of the great David" when they study his work.[5]

To understand the importance of what, to us, might seem a mere "poster" for a political convention, one must look into the political history of the state during the pre-Mexican War period, when the financial policy of the nation brought tempers to a boiling point.[6] In light of this, the artist was doing an important job for a vital cause and held up his usual criteria of performance.[7]

It must have been at about this time that there was excited in Bingham that intensive and extensive interest in the contemporary political scene. His dynamic and restless mind, combined with his determined and outspoken character, served him well for the controversies involved in the political strife; and we may rest assured that these controversies were not unwelcome to him. Because he became so vitally interested in affairs of state, and because the questions involved were of great significance to him, he plunged into the maelstrom with unabating vigor. We can see the artist-politician present at these meetings, speaking, engaging his friends in heated discussion, and, most important, turning his eye to the analysis of the stimulating variety of characters whom he saw about him. We can visualize him in a leisure moment, standing at a strategic vantage point, scrutinizing the assemblage and making many sketches of figures in their unself-conscious attitudes. "These sketches made at various times while he was making stump speeches, not only for others but for himself later when he was running for office, he worked into his compositions, which he painted in the studio, putting in the setting and arranging the compositions from memory plus imagination." [8]

Fortunately a splendid collection of these drawings which Bingham must have begun to make at about this period of his life is now in safe keeping in the Mercantile Library of St. Louis. The records of the library show that a Mr. John How presented the collection to the library in 1868. The drawings are now secured in a bound volume. In making a minute study and analysis of some of the genre work of Bingham, they are indeed a valuable assistance. All of these drawings are executed on a coarse manila paper, the foundation forms sketched lightly first in pencil and then worked over with a brush in either India ink diluted, or water color. All of the drawings range in size approximately from 8½ x 11 to 10 x 14. They are, happily, in a fine state of preservation.

Unquestionably these excellent testimonials to the superior ability of the artist as a draughtsman were sketched in pencil rather hurriedly and then worked over carefully in the studio with a brush. A minute examination of this series will reveal the uncanny dexterity of Bingham's hand, a swiftness of stroke, a sureness of line, and a delicacy of value contrasts which in some examples remind the observer of the inspired, thoughtful recklessness of a Daumier, the inimitable characterization of a Rowlandson, and the thoroughness of a Thomas Eakins.

This question has been raised: Why did Bingham become involved in politics, dissipating his energies in the later years of his life to the extent that his painting suffered, when he might have concentrated his thinking upon art and so made an even greater contribution to his time and his state? Now the answer to that query is simply this: Bingham was an activist. He could not stand by, as an observer, to watch the desecration of any principles which he, whose opinions were convictions, held over a wide range of interests.[9]

In his thirtieth year he writes to his Columbia friend that he would, indeed, prefer to devote his time and energies to painting; but he would, if necessary, leave the secluded life to throw himself into the fray of battle if that were needed to save the country.[10]

To Bingham's way of thinking, it always became necessary to leave the secluded life.[11] He was an Aristotelian: he believed that there are a thousand ways to be wrong, but only one way to be right.

Arthur Pope has written of Bingham as one of the last exponents of the Renaissance tradition of painting.[12] The artist's intellectual scope also recalls the spirit that dominated Leonardo, the man who, to many, personifies the essence of the Renaissance *Geist*.

Later in 1840 Bingham went to Washington, D. C., where he probably spent several years.[13] During this period in Washington he doubtlessly made several brief visits to various eastern centers. There is a record in the *Bulletin* of the American Art Union, August, 1849, which says that he remained in Washington nearly four years and that during that time he spent six months in Petersburg, Virginia. There are but two letters written to Rollins during his stay in the east and in neither does he give any definite information as to his residence in any other place but Washington. In the capital city his studio was located in a room of the then unfinished Capitol building. There was a great demand for portraits, for the politicians in Washington were probably eager that their countenances should be preserved for posterity as memorials to their eminence. Here

Bingham executed portraits of many a distinguished man of the age.[14]

Because Bingham was a deeply religious man and had studied the Bible with his characteristic thoroughness years before in Boonville,[15] he came to meet and win the friendship of a president of the United States.

Mr. Rollins tells the story that one day there entered into Bingham's studio a stranger who, after preliminary small talk, engaged the young portrait painter in a discussion of the Bible. It became evident that most of the information was on the side of the host, who so impressed the visitor with his erudition that the latter exclaimed: "Young man, if you know as much about painting portraits as you do about the Bible, you are an artist and I'll give you a sitting." In this way it came about that Bingham won the privilege of painting the portrait of John Quincy Adams. With typical honesty and a real modesty, Bingham refused Adams's offer of more money for the painting than was agreed upon. The artist was then only twenty-nine,[16] but already his intellectual interests had unlimited scope.

Bingham, now fully confident of his own abilities, gives further evidence of his scrupulous sense of fairness and honesty in a letter to Rollins.

"Washington City Dec 21, 1840

"Dear Sir

"Knowing you to be a friend to the Fine Arts I venture to intrude upon your attention a subject which otherwise I might hesitate to mention.

"Our splendid State house I believe is about completed, and I have been thinking that it would not detract from its fine architectural effect to have some suitable portion of the interior embellished with full length portraits of some two or three great men whose names are identified with the history of our country.

"The names of Washington, Jefferson, and Lafayette are held sacred by all parties, and in ordering their portraits, the state would not only evince a laudable regard for the arts, but a disposition to perpetuate the remembrance of these great benefactors of the human race.

"We have portraits of them here in the capitol, executed by the best masters of the art, from which faithful copies might easily be taken, at an expense merely nominal. And I should be glad if you would take so much interest in the subject as to propose it to the legislature now in session which might by resolution authorize the governor to employ an artist for such a purpose.

"Of course I should consider it an honor to receive such a commission from my own state, but do not desire it, unless it can be given upon a fair comparison of my merits as an artist with those of others who might be willing to engage in such work.

"The fact that the state of Illinois has just employed one of her own artists in a similar work, has led me to make the foregoing suggestion, and if you should see proper to act upon it in your legislative capacity, whether successful or not, you will add an additional obligation to many already received by

"Your Obt Servant
"Geo. C. Bingham

"J. S. Rollins esq
"P. S. please let me hear from you by letter as soon as convenient.
"G. C. B."

Meticulously honest as Bingham was, it is not surprising that his letter to Rollins does not insinuate that political influence might tip the balance of favor to himself. This disdain for political maneuvering characterized his private and political life; friend and foe alike recognized his integrity.

The Genre Paintings

SOMETIME in the early half of 1844, before Bingham left Washington, he had completed his first genre canvas, *Jolly Flatboatmen*.[1] In the year following, the painting was purchased by the American Art Union, and in 1846 a copy of an engraving appeared as a frontispiece of its journal.[2] This was described as the "best picture of that kind that had appeared in this country."[3] Bingham's reputation was much enhanced through this publicity, which spread among eastern artists; hereafter he was widely known as "The Missouri Artist."

Now there were at least three paintings of the subject *Jolly Flatboatmen*.[4] The painting from which was reproduced the engraving was owned by a B. Van Schaick of New York in 1847.[5] This painting has not been discovered since that date. The second painting, one found in Bingham's studio in 1879 and sold when the estate was dispersed in 1893, is no doubt that work which is now the property of Mrs. Thomas Mastin of Kansas City. This painting is unquestionably the painting of least merit.[6] The third, a larger composition, was painted in Germany in 1857.[7]

The original painting, from which was made the engraving, depicts eight figures seated on a raft, happily occupied in the enjoyment of the lively entertainment offered by three of their group. The fiddler (Figure No. 1) is enthusiastically scraping dance tunes from his instrument, simultaneously beating time with his left boot. From the drawing we can enjoy the uncanny accuracy of the artist in catching the spirit of animation which controls this musician. The folds of the loosely fitting shirt in their electric variety promote this sense of vigorous movement. The hands, actual masterpieces of good drawing, expertly produce spirited melodies from the fiddle. Completely alive and continuing the feeling of motion is the left leg and foot, which, lifted slightly, seems to be smartly transmitting the rhythmic tempo to the youthful lad beating the skillet (Figure No. 2).

The young accompanying artist is enjoying his responsibility hugely.

It is only to be regretted that Bingham did not see fit to follow in his painting his original sketches more exactly than he did; or that he was unable, as is the case with so many artists, to retain that spontaneity and freshness of conception during the process of transferring the spirit of the first drawing to his finished painted product. This is a fact, remarked now, which may be kept in mind throughout the further analysis of these sketches and paintings.

The skillet-beater, then, is a long haired, carelessly dressed, happy-go-lucky youngster who, with head tilted slightly toward the music, keeps time with his makeshift instrument. The drawing is a revelation of the adequately simple manner in which Bingham could transfer his ideas to paper with pencil and brush.

The youth (Figure No. 3) seated at the oar has been slightly altered in the painting to represent an older man. He is the only figure not apparently absorbed by the sport. Quite sardonically, arms resting on knees in a posture of complete relaxation, he gazes out into space. Probably the best portion of this drawing is revealed in the masterful treatment of the hands. The simple, two-value representation of the drooping left hand is excellently drawn.

A figure which, according to C. B. Rollins, is a passenger (Figure No. 4) on the flatboat watches the scene with intent and amused eyes. He seems to be the only member of the party who has paid some little attention to his appearance. The brush strokes revealing the folds of his vest and trousers are made with strong swift lines showing that unhesitating confidence which marks a practiced draughtsman.

Though in many cases the figures that Bingham sketched were used "verbatim" in his paintings, there are instances when a careful comparison will reveal slight discrepancies.

In a number of sketches which the writer examined in the Mercantile Library, St. Louis, the artist applied what appeared to be some cruder form of opaque water color, commonly known in our art classrooms today as "tempera" or show card color. The figure has had applied upon it some brush strokes of this opaque medium. It does not add greatly to the effect and seems to have been employed by Bingham only in cases where he made looser and less studied sketches.

Probably the next painting copied from the original is the painting now in the possession of Mrs. Thomas H. Mastin of Kansas City.[8] It may be deduced that this painting followed the original, for it is allied in composition to the engraving made after the initial painting. The dancer and the two musicians, however, are nearly exact forerunners of the three contained in the painting finished at Düsseldorf in 1857 (Plate XI, No. 1). After a minute inspection of a fairly clear photograph of the Mastin painting it might occur to the critic that there is something rather peculiar about this work. The drawing is disappointingly crude, the composition is naïvely pyramidal; and, above all, the value analysis is not that near-Dutch quality which usually characterizes Bingham at his best. Perhaps this painting was copied hurriedly to satisfy an impatient buyer. At some later date further information may reveal significant facts concerning the Mastin painting.

The work now owned by the Metropolitan Museum in New York, *Fur Traders Descending the Missouri* (Pl. III, No. 1), must have been painted sometime before 1844.[9] This canvas represents two figures in what was commonly termed a dugout. The veteran trapper, paddle in hand, seated in the rear of the canoe, is studied with the artist's usual care. The sketch (Figure No. 5) shows a more minute handling of the brush, portraying the character of a wild, untameable, and adventuresome voyageur. The face, weathered, lean and strong, with its eyes accustomed to penetrate long distance, is a revelation of character analysis. Easily and lithely he strokes the water, gripping the short canoe paddle in long-fingered, tenacious hands.

The figure of an unkempt youth (Figure No. 6) is shown slouched carelessly over the blanket-covered pile of supplies in the center of the canoe. The sketch shows him to be a wild-appearing boy, no doubt well fitted to win his livelihood in a sparsely settled wilderness with traps and a gun, which is held in readiness in his right hand. Here again Bingham employs in the treatment of the hair a delightfully spontaneous brush work. The folds of the garments in this sketch, as in nearly all of the drawings, are suggested by areas laid over with flat wash, and then modeled by strokes of the brush in cross-hatched lines, thereby acquiring texture and variation in the shading and shadow areas. Crouched in the forepart of the dugout is a dark-furred animal resembling a small bear. This is apparently a pet which has escaped the knife of the fur trader.

Shadowy in the background are the mysteriously outlined trees on the banks of the river. "The painting has a remarkable atmospheric quality which would be much more apparent were the old, discolored varnish removed. This quality is largely lost in the engraved or lithographic reproductions of the work of this period. This atmospheric rendering would seem to be less a convention than another evidence of Bingham's keenness of observation and feeling. Its quality is particularly appropriate for the soft brilliance of the humid atmosphere which is today characteristic of the Missouri Valley when untainted by coal smoke." [10]

By September 23, 1844, Bingham had returned to Boonville and begun to participate actively in political life, perhaps supporting himself and his family by portrait painting. To his friend he writes an interesting letter, referring to a previous request Rollins had made for a banner. He seems to be busily occupied doing similar works for two other counties [11] and describes in fairly exact terms his conception of a properly representative political banner.

"Boonville Sep 23 1844

". . . With reference to the banner which you desire for your delegation to our convention, I can merely state, that I shall be happy to execute it, provided you allow me to paint it on linnen, the only material on which I can make an effective picture.

"I am now just beginning one for Cooper, and one for Howard, each 7 by 8 feet—on one I shall give a full length portrait of Clay as the Statesman with his American System operating in the distance, on the other I shall represent him as the plain farmer of Ashland—each of them will also have appropriate designs on the reverse side, and will be so suspended, as to be easily borne by four men walking in the order of the procession. The cost will be from fifty to sixty dollars each.

"They will be substantial oil pictures and may be preserved as relics of the present political campaign.[12] If your delegation would be pleased with

[38]

FUR TRADERS DESCENDING THE MISSOURI

PLATE III
NO. 1

LANDSCAPE WITH CATTLE

PLATE III
NO. 2

a similar banner as "old Hal" is already fully appropriated I would suggest for the design as peculiarly applicable to your county, old Daniel Boone himself engaged in one of his death struggles with an Indian, painted as large as life, it would make a picture that would take with the multitude, and also be in accordance with historical truth. It might be emblimetical also of the early state of the west, while on the other side I might paint a landscape with 'peaceful fields and lowing herds' indicative of her present advancement in civilization.

"It would be full as large as those I am preparing for Cooper and Howard, and borne in the procession in like manner. If you approve of my suggestions or see proper to make others, write to me as soon as possible as I shall have but little time to spare.

"Yours Most respectfully,
"Geo. C. Bingham.

"Jas. S. Rollins, Esqr.
"P. S. On the reverse side of the Howard banner I intend to portray a large buffalo just broken loose from his keepers making the poke stalks fly to the right and left in the fury of his unbridled career."

On June 24, 1846, George Caleb Bingham was nominated Whig candidate for the Legislature from Saline County.[13] His opponent, the Democratic nominee, E. D. Sappington, contested the election after Bingham had been declared in office by a majority of three votes. After considerable litigation Bingham was forced to surrender his seat to his contestant. According to Mr. C. B. Rollins, "the contest was very laborious, and in the midst of it, Bingham gave vent to his irritation in a letter to my father." [14] This letter to Rollins, November 2, 1846, contains expressions of indignation which, now that the issue is hardly to be recalled except by students of the history of the locality, are pure entertainment.

"Marshall Nov 2, 1846

". . . If when you see me again you should not find me that pattern of purity which you have hitherto taken me to be, let the fact that I have been for the last four months full waist deep in Locofocoism plead something in my behalf. An angel could scarcely pass through what I have experienced without being contaminated. God help poor human nature. As soon as I get through with this affair and its consequences, I intend to strip off my clothes and bury them, scour my body all over with sand and water, put on a clean suit, and keep out of the mire of politics *forever*. (If you should be a candidate for the presidency, however, I may condescend to vote for you, or the next best Whig that may be presented.) . . ."

Inevitable in the early maturing strength of Bingham were traits of impatient bluntness which asserted themselves when he became provoked by differences of opinion. As a dogma lies at the basis of all action, so action is virile in exact proportion to the deep-seatedness of the dogma; as action is the result of belief, so the belief is revealed in the intensity of the act. With Bingham there was no half truth; he believed only in truth.[15] His acts, then, were sometimes violent, his pen frequently vitriolic and his painting, once at least, polemic.[16] Sappington's challenge tried Bingham beyond endurance. His speech before the House in 1846 is a gem of well-aimed and controlled ire.[17]

The American Art Union *Transactions* for 1846 [18] lists two paintings by Bingham, but unfortunately with no descriptions. They are *Boatmen on Missouri*, which came into the hands of J. R. Macmurdo, New Orleans, and *Landscape with Cattle*, to Charles Wilkes, Washington, D. C. It is possible that in the fire which destroyed the old Rollins home on Providence Road, Columbia, Missouri, 1908, the latter canvas was burned.[19]

On the other hand, the *Landscape* (Pl. III, No. 2) belonging to the City Art Museum of St. Louis may very plausibly be the canvas noted by Rusk as referred to by a newspaper in 1846 under the title *Landscape with Cattle*.[20] Something about the application of brush strokes over dark areas which, thus simply stippled, suggest the technique commonly employed by itinerant landscape painters who "do a work of art" in a few moments "for a dollar." This technique might have been more natural to Bingham in 1846 than in 1859 after he had become more experienced. It will probably remain a moot question, but it is not illogical to date this picture 1846.

A letter to Major Rollins dated March 10, 1847, indicates that Bingham spent at least the spring of that year in his home at Arrow Rock. Evidently still smarting under the previous Whig defeat, he writes encouragingly to his friend.

". . . Before I received your letter, I saw the published proceedings of your glorious Whig meeting in Jefferson, showing that there is still spirit enough left in our ranks, diminished as they are, to hurl defiance upon the foe, and fight for truth, justice, and our country. Judging from the resolutions adopted by the meeting, I think we will either conquer in the next campaign or *split our breeches.*

". . . Preferring the alternative presented in your letter, myself and wife have concluded to stay at home, and let yourself and wife and all that pertains thereto visit us. Let us know when to look for you that I may be at home at the time. . . ."

On April 21 there is a newspaper account which describes the two paintings *Lighter Relieving a Steamboat Aground* and *Raftsmen Playing Cards.*[21] The former painting was purchased in 1847 for $250 by a Mr. Yeatman of St. Louis. According to Rusk, it was sold again in 1849 to Mr. S. E. Paine, N. Y. Because this canvas has not been discovered we must be content with a brief description. "In the distance, aground on a sandbar, is a steamboat which has just been relieved of a portion of its cargo and the lighter or flatboat has been pushed out into the current, which carries it along without the use of oar or rudders. The flatboatmen are amusing themselves, some by listening to a tale of adventure told by one of their number, others by indulging in the contents of the jug and pipe. The newspaper further states that the characters are in their countenances, dress and attitudes 'true to life.' "[22]

Raftsmen Playing Cards

The second painting referred to in the St. Louis paper, *Raftsmen Playing Cards,* is without question the painting from which was made the lithograph. The description, in which is expressed the opinion that this is a better picture than *Lighter Relieving a Steamboat Aground,* discloses that two men are playing cards upon a raft floating with the current. One, seated astride a bench, apparently holds the high cards, while the other is "in a quandary" as to his next move. Two friends, one on either side of him, are suggesting which card he ought to play.

Now this description truly fits the lithograph. The painting from which this lithograph was reproduced must, therefore, be the original and must be really named *In a Quandary*. This canvas has never been located. The sound opinion can be advanced that *In a Quandary* was the original and that *Raftsmen Playing Cards*, now in the collection of the City Art Museum of St. Louis, is the second interpretation; the latter has incorporated in it the most absorbing qualities of the *Quandary* and has added to it more figures, all better drawn, in the second interpretation (Plate IV).

More evidence to this point is the account reported on August 17, 1847, by the *Jefferson City Metropolitan* concerning the notice found in a *New York Express* relating to the last production of "our favorite Missouri artist." The New York critic, attending the exhibit of paintings sponsored by the Art Union Collection, has written the following capricious criticism, which of course definitely dates the St. Louis painting as 1847 or perhaps a little before.

"The Jolly Raftmen, by G. C. Bingham—This is *almost a first rate* picture. It is truly American, (we always award this compliment with pleasure,) and decidedly original; and when we remember that the painter thereof is a statesman by profession, we think it a remarkable production. The scene represents a large plank which the artist has placed a number of raftmen. Two of them are playing cards on a wooden bench, while two of the party are looking on watching the progress of the game, one individual is seated on a plank examining his injured foot, while another is in the rear, hard at work managing the raft. The great merit of the picture consists in the decided character which distinguishes each individual. One of the players, rather a young man, whom we should designate a 'hard case,' has just thrown his card and is awaiting the result; while his antagonist, a somewhat older person and evidently a novice in the gambling art, is hesitating and troubled at the appearance of the game. The young man looking over his shoulder appears a mean and cunning scamp, probably the black sheep of a good family, and a sort of vagabond idler. The other person who is watching the progress of the players, is a middle aged man, industrious, frugal, and might be the respectable proprietor of the raft. The old fellow who is sitting on the plank and examining his sore foot, seems to be saying to himself with an oath—'No mistake about it, I've been long enough on the river, and the rolling of that log upon my foot the other day is a warning to me to give up this hard work; but what the devil shall I do? I haven't any money and no other way of getting it,—that's the question.' The man who is piloting the raft is undoubtedly thinking of his wife and children, and that is the reason he seems impatient to hurry on.

"The power of expression displayed in these figures is indeed remarkable, nearly, if not quite equal to Mount. The drawing of the picture, for the most part, and the design are graceful, though without much method. Of the coloring, however, we are disposed to complain. The flesh tints are all too heavy, and not in keeping with the surrounding effects of sunlight; the lights of the picture are too heavy and dead-like; and all the deeper shadows are nearly of one hue. The various accessories are equally touched in, but those in the immediate foreground are not sufficiently prominent to preserve the keeping, though they were probably subdued to help the figures. The sky of the picture is tame and uninteresting, but the landscape is true-nature in every particular. The monotonous shores of the Mississippi, with an occasional rocky headland, the rapid and muddy water, the characteristic snags and sand bars—all these are faithfully reproduced upon the canvass. Mr. Bingham is the only man in this country who has it in his power to rival Mr. Mount, but he must change the tone of his pictures. The field upon which he has entered is without a single superior in fruitfulness, and if he will only prove as faithful to that as Mount has to Long Island, his fondest anticipations, with regard to fame, will be fully realized.

"Mr. Bingham, tho' called the Missouri Artist, is not a native of Missouri. He was born in Virginia, and was a small boy in 1819 when his father emigrated to this State, and settled in Franklin, Howard county, where he died. If Mr. B. designs to distinguish himself as a painter, he ought to give up politics, about which he knows but little, and for which his peculiar temperament wholly unfits him."

The composition *Raftsmen Playing Cards* contains six figures. The center of interest is directed to the card players. The one to the left (Figure No. 7), evidently the "hard case," is superciliously watching the clumsy-minded calculation of his opponent. Right hand on thigh, the other, long and experienced, fingering three cards, presumably aces, he bends slightly forward, resting his left elbow upon his leg. He does not appear to be a raftsman himself, but probably is a passenger who is taking in the more naïve riverman. There is a slight error in the drawing of the right foot which has been completely altered and corrected in the painting. The texture of his garments show a better quality than those worn by his fellow player (Figure No. 8), who is puzzling slowly over his next play.

With lower lip protruding in a characteristic mannerism indicative of deep contemplation, the riverman is on the verge of venturing his next card. The frown and the lightly lifted ends of his eyebrows show his perplexed state of mind. The shoes, flat-soled, cheaply made, eloquently bespeak the owner's station. His trousers, too, seem baggy and ill-fitting. The shirt seems to be made of a coarse material. The artist deserves the compliment that in this figure also he obtains the feeling of solid structure beneath the garments.

The anatomy of Bingham's figures, no matter how difficult the position, is nearly always correct. Another remark about Bingham's drawing of hands would not be amiss: the suggestive manner with which this card player tentatively selects the card with his right hand is a tribute to Bingham's penetrating observational ability.

Standing duck-footed, watching the game is the figure of a younger man (Figure No. 9), probably posed by Dr. Oscar F. Potter, St. Louis, (Plate II, No. 2) who modeled for Bingham many times. The draughtsman who has studied much from life will doubly appreciate the accuracy and simplicity with which the feet are represented. Without faltering, the artist has drawn difficult passages and added suggestions even of veinous patterns. The values, too, are handled masterfully down to the last detail of reflected light. The grip of the left hand above the knee indicates the pressure exerted by the upper torso upon the arm. The folds of the trousers are pulled naturalistically correct and are drawn with deep, strong values. The face, in shadow, also speaks of Bingham's power to command delicately contrasting shades without losing the fundamental form.

With right foot resting on a barrel, the second attendant figure (Figure No. 10) is also evidently speculating as to the probable success or failure of his companion's next card play.

This figure, by the way, would suggest a certain explanation of the method by which Bingham worked to build his compositions. A comparison of this plate with the same figure in the canvas will reveal that the right leg is not shown in the painting. Neither is this leg completely drawn out in the sketch. Now, Bingham evidently followed an orthodox, common method of composition. He first designed his pictures roughly, briefly indicating according to compositional rule where the figures should be placed. If he had not previously made a life drawing, he posed the figure, made his finished drawing, and finally applied the essentials in his painting. Unfortunately, as mentioned before, Bingham did not always retain that spontaneous freedom in the transmission.

However, to return to the painting, the artist did superbly well in this canvas. Examining it more closely we see how faithfully Bingham has painted his various forms. The composition is obviously a pyramidal one with just enough variation to prevent monotony.[23] In the foreground a few still life studies verify his technical mastery of inanimate subject matter. The aerial perspective lends depth to the composition; and the sky, flat though it is, would not be criticized as being unnaturalistic by any who have lived along the Missouri River. Certainly the critic did not praise too highly in saying, "This is *almost a first rate picture.*"

Sometime during 1847 Bingham must have completed the *Old Field Horse,* "listed in Tuckerman's *Book of Artists* as belonging to the McGuire collection in Washington, D. C." [24] Nothing is known of this painting. The *St. Louis Republican,* November 28, 1847, contains a notice of a painting entitled *Lumbermen Dining. The Horse Thief* is mentioned by one of the earliest biographers of G. C. Bingham.[25]

The portrait of Oscar F. Potter (Plate II, No. 2), the friend of Bingham represented as the model for Bingham's *Raftsmen Playing Cards,* was executed in 1848. Most interesting is the noticeable change in technique which has developed in Bingham's portraiture within the past decade. Since 1835, the time that he painted his first known self-portrait, Bingham has known change and growth; he has been influenced by years of travel and by contacts with the art of the east and by his own accumulated experience.

The portrait of Potter shows a handsome physiognomy composed of alert and youthful eyes, brows nearly feminine in their shapeliness, a mouth sensitive and humorous—in brief, an attractive face showing intelligence and good breeding. The most obvious change in technique that this Bingham portrait shows is in the more smoothly connected planes, now no longer so sharply defined. To some artists this would not be considered an improvement, merely a change. It is true, however, that Bingham has now accumulated most of the conventional tricks of the trade and probably makes up in suavity what he has lost in unique and unspoiled individuality.

In the records of the American Art Union in 1848 is listed the title of another genre picture, important because it is probably the first one which depicts the political scene. The *Stump Orator*, assigned to William Duncan, Savannah, Georgia, has not yet come to light. It is interesting to speculate, however, whether some of the sketches contained in the Mercantile Library and reproduced in this volume are not the selfsame characters that occupied this canvas. Most likely to have been one of the figures in *Stump Orator* is the portly shape of a small-town politician speaking with feeble gestures to an assembled crowd of friends and neighbors (Figure No. 11). This drawing, obviously showing the antics of an amateur speaker, portrays a man of impressive weight and the kindly, embarrassed mien of a country bumpkin, lifting a pudgy finger to drive home what may be a poorly digested point of logic. Clothed in a shirt of homespun, coatless and with multiple-wrinkled trousers, the orator presents a most ludicrous appearance.

In examining this sketch we can readily believe that when a new political painting by Bingham was offered to the public view, there immediately was state-wide interest in the attempt to recognize and name each individual character. Some of them, indeed, who found themselves caricatured could not have been highly flattered. Consider, for example, that in the audience, pondering the eloquence of our speaker, is the country squire of magnificent expanse, seated upon what appears to be a stone wall (Figure No. 12). This respectable gentleman, cane in hand, left arm propped at a belligerent angle upon his knee, might be a landowner and employer personally interested in the affairs of state for financial reasons. The drawing, a masterpiece of technical handling, is a testimonial to the unyielding realism ever possessing Bingham, as well as a tribute to his cunning sense of humor. Only a man who had spent a lifetime among such folk could have so adequately represented this character.

Another citizen of undoubted worth is a side-whiskered rustic who seems to be amused as well as instructed by the speaker (Figure No. 13). Hat in hand, legs crossed, this individual is in a posture of listening. He is dressed quite formally for the occasion, no doubt feeling a bond of alliance to the other important and prosperous farmers and small town shop keepers. In this drawing the analysis of the left leg leaves something to be desired—it is too long; but, taken as a whole, the brush work has created a living personality.

For solidity of draughtsmanship none of the drawings can surpass the figure of the man seated in an attentive attitude, quietly weighing the veracity of the speaker's statements (Figure No. 14). In this posture Bingham shows his complete mastery of the problem of foreshortening. The right leg, with foot resting upon the top of the box on which he is sitting, is completely foreshortened. In the pencil basis the artist shows a few preliminary attempts to master this problem, has not erased the lines, and after satisfying himself that he is informed of the facts, sets out confidently with the brush to complete a perfect passage of drawing. Remarkable, too, is the muscular hand and veined arm which rests upon the knee.

Looking at this, the observer is likely to wonder at the amount of information which Bingham could absorb, simplify, and relate without hesitation with the pencil. No art school product has devoted more practice to conquering the problems of life drawing than Bingham must have expended to produce a drawing of such perfection. The face of this country gentleman, with its large, deep-sunken eyes, blunt nose, and generous mouth, is one typifying that spirit of rugged and intelligent manhood which, coming into a new country, conquered it and put its stamp upon it everlastingly.

Equally impressive as a character of marked power is the figure of an elderly gentleman smoking a long pipe, looking with wise, age-engraved face into the distance (Figure No. 15). He, too, may be one of the listeners; though too experienced to believe all that he hears, he is not cynical but almost sad. The hand which holds the pipe-stem is another example of expert drawing, as is the foot, drawn in detail in the lower left hand corner.

Intently engrossed in the message of his friend is the figure of a man sitting upon the ground (Figure No. 16). He is gazing upward, evidently pleased by what he hears. The drawing of the left arm holding the hat is a beautifully modeled section of brush work. Following the form with the intuition of a sculptor, Bingham gives a nearly uncanny sense of roundness to the upper arm. The folds, studied accurately, are nevertheless treated simply, and the drawing is always tied together with a knowingly applied layer of foundation wash.

One can only ruminate the question as to the amount of time it took the artist to finish any one of these sketches, but in a close examination of the original works the writer was lead to believe that each drawing was rapidly executed in pencil without many hesitant strokes and then speedily developed in the studio from his memorized knowledge of form and chiaroscuro. Drawn in this manner, the figures discussed above possibly appeared in *Stump Orator*, painted in 1848 and never since brought to the public eye.

In 1848 Bingham was once more candidate for the House of Representatives, running on the Whig ticket. In this election he was completely vindicated. E. D. Sappington, his old opponent who had early ousted him from his seat in the Legislature, was defeated. During Bingham's tenure of office he was appointed upon the committee on Federal Relations and the committee on Enrolled Bills. He conducted himself with credit in all his duties and "it was said by some of his friends" fifteen years later "that his great speech against secession was the first defiant utterance against rebellion in the Capitol in Missouri." [26]

Shortly after Bingham's election to the Legislature, his wife, to whom he had been married twelve years, died. The *Missouri Statesman*, December 29, 1848, contains the following obituary notice. "Deaths:—In Arrow Rock, Missouri, Mrs. Sarah Elizabeth Bingham, wife of George Caleb Bingham, Esq. of Saline county, aged 29 years."

Despite official duties and personal bereavement, Bingham must have been busy during all this time with his brush and palette. The *St. Louis Missouri Republican*, April 17, 1849, contains the following brief description of three paintings:

"Yesterday we had the pleasure of examining three paintings by G. C. Bingham, Esq., who is better known by the sobriquet above given—albeit he is not unknown as a statesman and politician. In his peculiar line of Western characters he has added three gems to the productions of his pencil. One is a scene in a bar-room, in which the group is most perfect and lifelike. The jolly old landlord, smoking his pipe; a politician, most earnestly discussing to a very indifferent listening farmer, the Wilmot Proviso; whilst a boy, with his coat-tail turned up to the stove, is reading a show-bill. Another is a picture drawn from our own wharf, in which he has introduced a true and life-speaking description of some of the scenes which may be daily witnessed there. It is the first painting which we have in which the real characteristics of the boatmen on the wharf are truly portrayed. Another, which is a gem, is a 'woodyard' in which there is a true artistical representation of a scene on the Missouri. The owner of the woodyard, and his laborers, are awaiting the arrival of a boat, and their anxiety to make a sale of their wood is strikingly delineated. It is a most complete picture of Western life."

Named in the order in which they are described in the contemporary newspaper article, these three paintings are probably *County Politician*, *St. Louis Wharf*, and *Woodyard*.

The first of these three paintings was assigned to John Boyd, Winsted, Connecticut, in 1849, and nothing has been heard of it since that time.[27] *St. Louis Wharf*, won by S. Pell, New York, in the same year, is also still missing.[28] However, there are some sketches in the Mercantile Library collection which, like those described as being the probable figures employed in *Stump Orator*, are material for absorbing speculation. In this painting, as the brief description states, the true character of the rivermen is portrayed. Now, as the attitudes of most of the sketches are self-revelatory as to the subject's profession, his character, and his immediate interest, so these few drawings, too, distinctly differ from the "political scene type" and may be prototypes of figures Bingham placed in the "wharf scene" canvas.

The disreputable, unkempt and bepatched riverman (Figure No. 17) is very probably one of those transient citizens who frequented the river bank. He is seated, ambitionless, gazing with that vacancy which is often found in the long stare of the empty-minded. Battered hat cocked over a thatch of unbrushed hair, a week's growth of whiskers covering a face that is weak-jawed and unspirited, he appears to be an individual who takes what he can with beaten resignation. The discouraged look in his eyes, with their half drooping lids, is made more pathetic by a worried frown which distorts his forehead. The listless drop of his left hand shows what character Bingham could work into an attitude, whether that attitude involved the whole figure or merely a portion. The patched trousers lend the last touch of description to this impecunious drifter.

The sleeping tramp (Figure No. 18) leaning his head upon what is probably a parcel of cargo upon the wharf, is even more discouraging than the one just described. With open mouth he is snoring away his time in the warm sun. It was at the time of Giotto that painters began, in occidental pictorial art, to turn their attention to "attitudes." We read, for instance, of the attitudes of the mourners at the bier of St. Francis in the painting by the great Florentine. Bingham, with his scientific and examining eye, no doubt studied the attitudes of his contemporaries and remarked the difference between the abject sag of the hobo as compared with the self-important strut of the property-owning respectable. The sleeping derelict represented here suggests, in every line, his true self. The relaxed hands impart the impression of sleep. The shoulders rest unconsciously upon the support of the canvas covered box. The hat shading the face has gone askew, pushed back by the right arm of the sleeper.

Looking up with some belligerence, another "tough" character (Figure No. 19) is probably watching some activity upon the wharf. Seated on

[50]

the planks, he humps stoop-shouldered against his knees. Bingham has drawn him with swift lines, imparting a sense almost of menace, which some of the wharf loafers probably possessed. In the upper right hand corner of the sketch, there is drawn in, with great surety, a hand supporting an arm upon a roundish object. In so many of these incidental notations the artist has worked with a freedom of line and an economy of detail which is an indication of his sure capability with the pencil and brush.

The third painting described in the article, *Woodyard*, has, like the others, not been discovered.

Listed in the American Art Union *Transactions* for 1849 are two paintings entitled *A Boatman* and *Raftsmen on the Ohio*. The first, showing "a figure seated upon a pile of wood on the banks of the Missouri," [29] was ascribed to "J," a resident of Albany, New York. The *Raftsmen*, also distributed by the Art Union in 1849, came into the possession of a James Key of Florence, Alabama. The brief description in the *Bulletin* says that "a man seated on a box is telling a story to three others as they are floating down the Ohio. In the foreground on the raft are packs of shingles, boards, etc." [30]

With only the brief sentence of description to guide us as to the nature and activity of the characters represented in *Raftsmen on the Ohio*, we again build up an imaginary composition employing three of the sketchbook figures as the characters within our picture. The figure seated upon a wood block (Figure No. 20) seems to be reciting an entertaining tale to his companions, who are watching him intently (Figures No. 21 and 22). The story teller, with pointed finger, is bringing forth unquestionable evidence to substantiate the truth of what he says. He appears to be quite serious in his art, but he does not take in his two listeners, who are hiding their smiles of incredulity behind crooked fingers. The expressions on the faces of this trio are excellent character revelations. Again it is pleasant to see the complete mastery of drawing that Bingham shows in depicting the skeptical figure (Figure No. 21) who is looking at the man telling the story.

Watching the Cargo

Also in 1849 Bingham painted *Watching the Cargo* (Plate V, No. 1). Fortunately in a perfect state of preservation, this canvas is hanging in the reading room of the Missouri Historical Society, Columbia, Missouri. It depicts three figures evidently keeping watch over a cargo of freight which has been removed from a grounded steamboat and placed on the bank of the Missouri River. Because the Missouri River from St. Louis to Boonville was a span precarious for steamboats, the scene doubtless is one that Bingham witnessed somewhere near his old home in Franklin.

The most striking personality of the three men shown in this picture, is seated on a box staring intently ahead, smoking a long pipe (Figure No. 23). Attention must be directed to the beautifully drawn boots. The foreshortening is admirably accomplished; and above all, in this simple direct method, the artist has conveyed the solidity and texture of these sturdy, waterproof brogues. The figure is resting solidly upon the cargo box, legs crossed, one arm resting idly in his lap, the other with hand loosely holding the unique pipe. Scraggly brows cover piercing eyes which stare out above well-defined, high-placed cheek bones. The wide generous mouth, with stubborn lower lip supported by a prominent chin, gives an unusual effect of arresting distinction.

It is helpful to note in this drawing that even in his sketches Bingham devoted careful attention to the problem of chiaroscuro, as is obviously noticeable in his paintings.

Sprawled on the ground before this figure is a broad-faced man, a good-natured yokel (Figure No. 24) who is leisurely sharing the responsibility of guarding the stack of supplies. Probably most worthy of comment in this sketch is the remarkable manner in which the draughtsman has drawn the left hand dangling relaxed from the support of his raised left knee. A most subtle variation of values places the hand in its proper plane, setting it off against the background of the knee. This passage, handled so craftily, is but another illustration of Bingham's superior drawing ability. The slouch in the torso is pronounced, giving to the

[52]

subject an easy relaxation. The face of this man, wide, side-burned, good-natured, is remarkably different from that of his companion. The straw hat, beautifully shaped and thoroughly modeled, is a paragon of drawing technique.

Just back of the first mentioned figure is a youth blowing the first feeble sparks of a newly-laid fire. Completely absorbed in his efforts, he crouches, concentrated, before the split log and branches. The composition uses as an expedient the ancient compositional device of mass balanced by distance. The eye escapes from these figures and their cargo on the left of the picture, down the river winding gradually into a hazy distance. Some distance down the river we see the stranded steamboat lurching slightly, jammed into a sandbar. The sky is a nicely defined pattern of light grayed tonalities and indicates Bingham's careful and astute observation of nature.[31]

In 1849 during August and September Bingham visited again in New York. His studio was located at 115½ Grand Street, and the Art Union advertised his series of sketches, which were on exhibition. The *Bulletin* of the American Art Union for August, 1849, contains a notice of the visit of the Missouri Artist to New York "and other eastern cities."

"THE BULLETIN OF THE AMERICAN ART-UNION for August contains the following notice of GEORGE C. BINGHAM, 'THE MISSOURI ARTIST,' who is now on a professional visit to New York and other eastern cities:

" 'A clever picture by Bingham, the Missouri Artist, has been added to the purchases since our last publication. One or two other works by him will probably be upon exhibition during the present month, and attract much attention by the fidelity of their representations of Western life and manners. Most of our readers may remember the "THE JOLLY FLAT BOATMEN" which was engraved for the subscribers in 1847, as well as the "RAFTSMEN PLAYING CARDS," and the STUMP ORATOR," which were included in late distributions, and greatly admired, were from the easel of this artist. All these works are thoroughly American in their subjects, and could never have been painted by one who was not perfectly familiar with the scenes they represent. It was this striking nationality of character, combined with considerable power in form and expression, which first interested the Art-Union in these productions, notwithstanding the existence of obvious faults. This assistance of the Society was of material importance to the artist. Indeed, according to his own statement, if it had not been bestowed, he would never perhaps have attempted that peculiar class of subjects which have given him all his reputation.—It is pleasant to see that this encouragement was properly bestowed, and that observation and study have already corrected, to a considerable degree, those defects in color, in the distribution of light and shadow and in specific form, which formerly diminished the value of his works; while the higher qualities of character and expression and general form which first attracted the attention of the Committee, are still preserved. His figures have some VITALITY about them. They look out of their eyes. They stand upon their legs. They are shrewd or merry or grave or quizzical. They are not mere empty ghosts of figures—mere pictures of jackets and trowsers, with masks attached to them. . . .' " [32]

According to this evaluation, the critic who wrote this account has improved his opinion of Bingham since the latter's previous visit to the metropolis. Bingham, by this time, had definitely "arrived."

By the latter part of September the artist was at work in Columbia upon the portraits of Dr. William Jewell,[33] Dr. Lathrop, president of the University of Missouri (a portrait which was destroyed by fire in 1892),[34] and probably other persons of lesser prominence.

The *Missouri Statesman*, December 7, 1849, contains the following notice: "*Marriages*—In this place on sabbath morning last (the 2nd inst.) at 10 o'clock, by Elder W. W. Keep, Mr. *George C. Bingham*, "the Missouri artist," of Arrow Rock, to Miss *Eliza*, daughter of Prof. Robert S. Thomas, of this place." Bingham's second wife "is said to have been beautiful and intelligent, and an excellent mother to her husband's children." [35]

In 1850, judging from a contemporary account,[36] Bingham was working in St. Louis. "Mr. George C. Bingham, 'the Missouri Artist,' at his studio in this place is about completing, for George W. Austen, Esq., of New York, Treasurer of the American Art Union, one of the choicest specimens of art with which we have met. It is a fair conception and most graphically delineated. The painting represents a western scene— *Shooting for the Beef*—and presents a group of characters with life-like fidelity.[37] There are seen the eager marksmen in the attire of the backwoodsman; the log cabin at the cross-roads, with sign above the door lintel, 'Post Office Grocery;' the prize in contest, a fat ox, chained to a stump hard by; a beautiful landscape in prospective, and—but a description is impossible. The painting is thirty-six by forty-nine inches. Every feature on the canvas is instinct with life. Indeed it seems an incarnation rather than painting, and gives us reason to exult in the genius of Bingham, a native Artist of our own state." [38]

Shooting for the Beef, after being purchased by the Art Union, was auctioned, because in 1852 the system of raffling paintings had been declared contrary to the statutes of New York State prohibiting lotteries. [39] This painting (Plate VI, No. 1), now in the F. P. Garvan Collection, is signed in the lower left-hand corner and dated 1850. It is in an excellent state of preservation. It is questionable whether Bingham had prepared for the painting of this picture by making sketches of the figures with his usual care. At least none of the figures of these sportsmen are to be found in the sketchbook. A special examination of this canvas brings to attention the fact that many of the figures are not drawn with the artist's usual crispness; a "broad" quality is to be noticed, which is to be found in only one other of the genre paintings, "Order No. 11." Bingham painted both pictures, evidently, more hurriedly than was his habit. At the auction sale held by the Art Union there were included the following paintings: "*Cattle Piece* (36 x 26¼)—Oxen and cows feeding on a meadow." "*Fishing on the Mississippi* (36 x 26)—Three men are stationed on the rocks at the left, engaged in this sport. A flatboat is coming down the stream." "*The Squatters* (30 x 25)—A family has built its log cabin in the midst of a clearing, and commenced housekeeping." "*The Wood-Boat* (30 x 25)—The boat is drawn up to the shore. The boatmen are resting themselves on the banks." "*Trapper's Return* (36 x 26)—The figures are descending the river in a dig-out, at the bows of which is a bear, chained." [40] These were probably paintings that Bingham had sold to the Art Union during a visit in New York during the winter of 1850–1851.

It seems impossible to find the originals of these paintings except for *Fishing on the Mississippi*.

Fishing on the Missouri

The second painting mentioned among those sold, *Fishing on the Mississippi,* is either lost or it is the *Fishing on the Missouri* which is now owned by the William Rockhill Nelson Gallery in Kansas City, Missouri (Plate V, No. 2). If there are the two, *Fishing on the Mississippi* must have been painted a few months earlier than the *Fishing on the Missouri,* because the former as mentioned above was presumably purchased from Bingham in New York and was therefore painted sometime during 1850. The painting *Fishing on the Missouri* is signed 1851.[41]

This canvas shows three fishermen, with a dog, fishing from the rocky ledge of the river. A stream of sunlight has flooded that portion of the rock where they are located, setting off the three men with sharp distinction against the dark weight of the background bluffs. The eye of the observer, after studying the three sportsmen, passes on into the picture, ushered into the background by the strong line of the rugged bluffs lining the shore.

Finally, progress is interrupted by the view of three raftsmen plying the long oars of a flatboat which is coming down the stream. To connect further the raftsmen with the figures on the ledge, Bingham has with some cleverness pointed the fishing pole of the central figure directly from ledge to boat. The tall figure in the immediate foreground, baiting his hook (Figure No. 25), is drawn rather carefully with flat wash laid over the shaded portions and then stroked in cross-hatching to lend fullness and life. The hands are thoroughly analyzed and represented with exacting faithfulness. The line quality is strong and definite. In the painting this figure has been duplicated with hardly any alteration.

Chin in hand, the figure reclining upon a rock (Figure No. 26) is evidently examining some scene on the farther shore. Certainly he is not attending to his fishing. The sketch is more loosely done, the rocks suggested very briefly, and the coat upon which he has pillowed his elbow is barely shaped. Again, as in the *Raftsmen Playing Cards* (Plate IV), this sketch helps us to see exactly how Bingham developed his compositions. Since the legs of this individual are not shown in the painting, one assumes that the artist did not bother to sketch them, being content to concentrate his work upon the torso and head.

At first thought it might seem that the last painting on the Art Union list, *Trapper's Return*, has been confused with an earlier work, *Fur Traders Descending the Missouri*,[42] because the description of *Trapper's Return* fits exactly the painting now owned by the Metropolitan Museum. However, since the Metropolitan purchased their painting through the descendants of R. S. Bunker, to whom *Fur Traders* was attributed in 1845, it is definitely established that *Trapper's Return* is a variant of the earlier painting.[43]

From St. Louis, Bingham went to New York in the fall of 1850. In March, 1851, Bingham wrote to his friend:

"New York March 30, 1851

". . . You wish to know what I am doing. I am now painting The Emigration of Boone and his Family to Kentucky. I do not know whether I will sell it to one of the art unions, or have it engraved with the expectation of remunerating myself from the sale of the engravings. The subject is a popular one in the West, and one which has never yet been painted. One of my recent pictures of life upon the Mississippi [44] will be engraved this year in Paris by Goupil and Co., a French publishing house, a branch of which is located in this city. I have engaged to paint another for them in the course of the summer.[45] Their publication by such a firm will be calculated to extend my reputation and enhance the value of my future works. I have discovered since I have been here that the present managers of the art union display in some cases gross favoritism in the purchase of their pictures, and in my transactions with them hereafter, I shall act as if I were dealing with a Jew. I sent three pictures to Philadelphia this winter, two of them sold very readily, the other not being a well-selected subject I intend to keep. The pictures I painted last year are all sold with the exception of the checker players . . ."

The last two sentences of this letter indicate that *Cattlepiece*, *Fishermen on the Mississippi*, *The Squatters*, *The Wood-Boat*, *Trapper's Return*, and *Chess Players* may have been painted in 1850.

The painting, *The Emigration of Boone and His Family to Kentucky*, to which Bingham devoted his time in New York during the spring of 1851, is not the same canvas, identically, which we know today as probably his most popularly publicized work, *Daniel Boone Coming Through the Cumberland Gap* (Plate VI, No. 2).

The original conception, from which Goupil and Company made their engraving, pictured an altogether different background arrangement. Daniel Boone surrounded by the three figures most prominent in the picture, horse, dog, and immediate foreground, are the only aspects of this initial composition which remain exactly the same in the repainted version. There is no question, however, that the painting owned by Washington University, St. Louis, is the original canvas with background revised, because the underpainting, as years pass, shows through more clearly and reveals passages of the original interpretation.[46]

There is some question as to whether this work should be considered genre or historical painting. The heroic, majestic background of the revised painting has suggested to some the influence of the Hudson River School. The opinion of Mr. James Musick of the City Museum, St. Louis, is that the Hudson River School had not much to give to Bingham, for the latter's landscape is more powerful and "would seem to show the superiority of Bingham's work in solidity and power of conception." [47]

Daniel Boone, with wife, daughter, and companions, leads the procession of pioneers through the gap in the Cumberland Mountains. Boone, eyes alertly ahead, gun in readiness, seems to be ever watchful for danger that may threaten his daring adventurers. His light yellowish, homemade garment stands out in high relief against the more somber garb of the man immediately behind him. The magnificent animal which he leads with his right hand is carrying Boone's wife, Rebecca, a woman of apparent courage and equal determination. Just behind her, white-shawled, can be distinguished the face of his intrepid daughter, Jemima, also a bold pioneer. Behind these major characters comes the procession of friends who have entrusted their fortunes into the hands of their gallant

WATCHING THE CARGO

Plate V
NO. 1

FISHING ON THE MISSOURI

Plate V
NO. 2

leader. Rising grandly on either side of the cavalcade are the lofty mountains, somber, lowering, colossal. The last dim lines of the retreating crags meet a sky dramatically cloud-blown.

To the left of Daniel Boone is a figure (Figure No. 27) which is said by Mr. C. B. Rollins to be Flanders Callaway, who later married Jemima Boone, daughter of the noted frontiersman. He strides forward with a heroic and grim determination. Gun in hand, with munition pouch swung over his left shoulder, he seems in the sketch to be a worthier hero than the final painting would show him to be.

Leaning forward to adjust a moccasin, the figure (Figure 28) to the right of the dramatically portrayed charger is a guide whose identity has not been made known by any source. The sketch shows pencil lines which Bingham employed to adjust the action and proportions of his models, over which have been laid very freely the brush strokes.

"In June, 1853, Bingham was exhibiting the picture in St. Louis. He proposed to dispose of it by raffle. Three hundred shares were to be sold at two dollars each, as the work was valued at six hundred dollars; two hundred of the chances had already been taken. It was just the year previous to this, as we have seen, that the American Art Union's method of distribution by lot was condemned. But most people did not feel averse to this kind of lottery, and it was even urged (we do not know whether the suggestion was followed) that the literary societies of the University purchase a number of shares, so that they might stand a good chance of obtaining the *Emigration of Daniel Boone* for the University."[48] The quotation from Rusk can be substantiated by a portion of a letter which Bingham wrote to Rollins from St. Louis on March 9, 1853.[49] "I have the *Emigration of Boone* in charge of Mr. Phillips the pianoforte merchant. He thinks he will be able to dispose of all of the tickets in two or three weeks and will then see that the drawing is properly conducted."

County Election

We find Bingham again in Columbia by May of 1851,[50] where he spent the next six months busily occupied painting upon a number of important genre subjects, among which were *County Election* and *Canvassing for a Vote*. Though the first painting devoted to the portrayal of the Missouri political scene, named *Stump Orator*, is known to have been painted before 1848, these two canvases, as far as we know, are the first of a series of political genre. It is upon this series and upon the "river life" series that Bingham's claim to fame will probably rest.

The large canvas, *County Election*, is composed of over sixty figures and occupied about three months of this period. A revealing account in the *Missouri Statesman*, October 31, 1851, speaks of the work in his studio.

"We had the pleasure a few days since of visiting Mr. Geo. C. Bingham, 'the Missouri Artist,' at his studio in this place, and examining several new and exquisitely executed oil paintings—works of art which are destined to add additional lustre to his well-earned fame.

"The first which fell under our observation, and the most prominent was, *the day of election*. This picture has engaged the artist constantly for three months, occupies canvass about three by four feet, and is composed of upwards of sixty figures. Prominently on the right, on the main street of a western village, we have the place of voting, the court house, in the porch of which the clerks and judges are assembled—one of the judges, a thick pussy looking citizen, being engaged in swearing a voter, a well-set Irishman in a red flannel shirt. Near by is a political striker, a distributor of tickets, *very* politely tendering his services in that regard to an approaching voter. Around and in front is the crowd, composed of many large and prominent figures— some engaged in earnest conversation, some drinking at a cake and liquor stand, some smoking and some hearing a paragraph read from a newspaper. But we cannot give a description of this painting. Several hours would not suffice fully to examine it, so numerous and life-like are the characters. Indeed it is full of reality, a seeming incarnation, prominent in figure, grouped and colored with admirable skill and effect. Persons of highly cultivated taste in the fine arts, and critics in general, will accord to it a remarkable degree of genius and merit.

"There was also in his studio a smaller painting, another political scene of great originality of conception and beauty of finish, to wit: CANDIDATE ELECTIONEERING. We likewise examined the CHESS PLAYERS, and a very beautiful landscape SCENE ON THE OHIO. All these paintings are executed with a master's hand, and are well worthy the examination of connoisseurs of the art. The political scenes are original and bold, and present a class of subjects entirely new.

"Mr. Bingham we understand intends taking these paintings to St. Louis, where he will spend the winter."

The painting named by the reporter "the day of election" is, of course, the popular and widely known work *County Election*. (Plate VII).

Until 1937 the painting described above was commonly held to be the canvas now owned by the Mercantile Library and displayed in the St. Louis City Museum. Fern Helen Rusk raised the question in 1914 as to whether this painting was the original or a replica. She states that this painting, together with three other canvases of the Election Series, was given to the Library "by John H. Beach, who was then President of the Library Board. He had bought them from Bingham upon the advice of A. J. Conant, an artist and a friend of Bingham's, whom the latter had asked to help in selling the pictures. It seems hardly probable that Bingham would have had the picture again in ten years after it had been sold in Kentucky, and yet the one in the Mercantile Library agrees quite perfectly with the engraving."

The engraving, however, agrees altogether with the newly discovered *County Election*. The most obvious agreement is this: In Mr. Rollins' picture and in the engraving there are no figures immediately above and behind the trio of men, engrossed in serious conversation, in the right lower part of the painting. In the later Mercantile Library-owned painting, two figures have been added. Furthermore, the sky treatment and the tree foliage in the Rollins' painting and in the engraving are quite identical.

"Again in 1879 the *County Election* was mentioned in a list of paintings then in the artist's studio. And in May, 1895, a painting referred to as *'Election Day in Independence, Missouri*—an illustration of western life before the war,' was on exhibition and offered for sale in Boston. So there must have been at least one replica and probably two." There is no evidence available which would indicate that the last-mentioned painting, *Election Day in Independence, Missouri,* was a scene such as depicted in *County Election.* But Rusk's argument is well taken.

Since 1923 Mr. C. B. Rollins had suspected that the initial painting of the *County Election* was not the one which is housed in the City Museum. It was his belief that this canvas had been stored in a warehouse in Louisville, Kentucky.[51]

A thorough investigation of certain transactions which involved the *County Election* brought several facts to light. Robert J. Ward purchased the painting (see letter) from the artist himself. After Ward's death, his widow, Mrs. Ward, had sold the picture to one Mr. Irvine, a wealthy steamboat operator. Irvine, in turn, willed the canvas to his wife, who, being a devout Presbyterian, presented it to her pastor, the Reverend Dr. Charles J. Hemphill, Dean of the Presbyterian Theological Seminary.

In 1926 Mr. Rollins visited Dr. Hemphill with the intention of purchasing the *County Election* for the University of Missouri. Because the committee could not agree upon a purchase price, however, the sale was not effected.

In 1931, Mr. James Hemphill, son of the minister, wrote to Rollins, stating that he was willing to dispose of the canvas for a reasonable sum.

During an unsuccessful trip which Mr. Rollins made to Louisville in 1934, he was told that the *County Election* had been lost. Hemphill and Rollins went over to the Brook's Warehouse, where the picture was stored, to see the painting. It could not be located at that time. Leaving instructions that he was to be informed if the canvas were found, Mr. Rollins returned to Columbia.

In May, 1937, he received from Hemphill the happy news that the *County Election* had been discovered. The Brook's Warehouse Company had been sold to a larger concern, which had ordered the transference of certain storage properties from one building to another. In this moving,

PLATE VI
NO. 1

SHOOTING FOR THE BEEF

THE EMIGRATION OF BOONE

PLATE VI
NO. 2

the well-crated picture, wrapped in canvas and protected by paper, was disclosed.

The original political scene (Plate VII) was purchased by Rollins in May of 1937 and shipped by him to Columbia, Missouri, where it was hung in the library of his home. It is there today, one of the most prized possessions of the son of the greatest friend and patron of the artist.

A careful comparison of the engraving (Plate VIII, No. 2) to the Rollins' painting (Plate VII) and the Mercantile Library painting (Pl. VIII, No. 1) will be interesting. The differences and similarities will be noticed.

Because Bingham was not in any way influenced by the contemporary French painters, it is not surprising that he is today found to be, by those who derive their criteria of judgment from the nineteenth century schools of French painting, lacking in the effective use of hues. Certainly he did not subscribe to, even if he knew of, such methods of working pigment as were advanced and employed by Parisian painters or by the Barbizon artists. From Bingham's writings there are no evidences whatsoever that he gave serious consideration to the highly aesthetic theorists who were saying things about "plastic" or "functional" use of color.

No doubt a more conscious concern of color would have been of help to Bingham. As it was, the Missourian followed a strictly conventionalized system of painting, which grew quite naturally out of his paramount concern with representation. After his drawing and design had been wed, and his value patterns arranged to his satisfaction, Bingham set out to color his canvas with meticulous, methodical care.

A set of the artist's brushes, treasured by the Morrison Hughes family of Fayette, Missouri, is evidence of his careful concern for detail. Each brush is small, delicately pointed, and most of them are handmade with sable hair and bristle, goose quill and pine wood. Bingham used such delicate instruments with which to cover his canvas and, of course, these could not possibly be manipulated in a broad manner. It was by a series of form-following strokes, patiently applied, that Bingham modeled his figures, fashioned the foliage, and formed the architecture upon his canvases.

[63]

An intimate examination of the colors in a Bingham picture (see plates in color) will disclose such an intricate arrangement of brush strokes, such fidelity to minutiae, as to amaze the observer. It is not surprising that the painter found it necessary to devote many months to the painting of one of his larger genre pictures.

Mary Morsell, editor of the *Art News*, has come exactly to the point in saying, "The color sense of the mid-nineties was not subtle and save in a few instances Bingham seems to have meekly followed the general predilection for hearty pinks and blues and greens, easily translatable into the popular color prints of the period. This, at first glance, slightly obscures for the average visitor the more solid virtues of the paintings on view." [52] At least this generalization covers pretty thoroughly the majority of Bingham's works.

In *Raftsmen Playing Cards* the artist has done his finest color work. Here there is blended into smooth harmonies a limited palette of hues, developed with the painter-like quality of a master. And in a few portraits Bingham attained clear, yet subdued hues which delight the eye.

Thomas Benton has frequently marveled at the purity and quality of the whites which Bingham used. "Not many painters today," remarked Benton, "can retain such clarity in their whites for even five or ten years."

Observed from a distance of a few feet, the colors, even though usually "hearty pinks and blues," blend and become subordinate to the design unity of the whole.[53]

That "Bingham must have gotten his lessons in composition from engravings after Renaissance-Baroque masters" [54] is suggested by this impressive canvas *County Election* (Plate VII). The screen of architecture extending from the upper right-hand corner down into the distant axis of the design speaks reminiscently of many masters of the Renaissance.[55] A stream of light striking from the left reveals in sharp contrast all of the figures of major importance. Upon this light arrangement the eye swings back and forth from the negro freedman, who dispenses the election drinks to thirsty patrons, across a group of intermediate figures up to the center of interest, the Irish-looking bumpkin who is being sworn by the pompous judge. This constitutes the first plane of the composition.

In immediate parallel to it are the subordinate figures, giving background and incidental points of interest to the picture. These characters have been painted in grayed intensity, low value terms and, though absorbingly interesting when studied in detail, they by no means project themselves, unbehaved, into the order of the first plane. The third line of figures, lowered in value to the extent that the figures appear silhouetted against the far background, gives a solid support to the forelying groups and serves technically as a dark background against which the artist can obtain sufficient contrast so as not to lose his second plane forms. Then, in the distance, the lighting is again repeated, illuminating architectural structures. This repetition is an obvious expedient to invite the eye into the full depth of the canvas. The sky is handled in a well-designed, unostentatious fashion.

Often an artist who, like Bingham, "goes to nature" for his inspiration is stamped by order-minded critics as simply "naturalistic." Now Bingham has been casually designated as belonging to the category of "photographic" artists. A conscientious perusal of Bingham's works may convince the critic, however, that Bingham cannot be catalogued accurately as naturalistic. In spirit he seems more closely allied to a modern Benton than to any so-called naturalist. Anyway, Mr. Marquis Childs gives us something upon which we should reflect. "It is perhaps time to re-examine the term 'photographic art,' for it would seem that the veriest hack, who wants to achieve photography, adds something that no mechanical recording device could ever add, something that is inherent in the time." [56] Bingham can be defined more accurately as a "realist."

Luckily, the Mercantile Library sketchbook contains fifteen drawings of figures employed in the creation of this political canvas, *County Election*. As we identify the drawings with those within the picture from left to right, the negro freedman (Figure 29) is studied first. The sketch indicates the fact that the artist sometimes did not adhere in every detail to the preliminary study he made for his composition. The smiling negro, though in the exact position which was later transcribed to the canvas, is minus the hat and apron which Bingham later painted in. The negro, highly pleased with the importance of his job and grinning broadly, is in the act of pouring another glassful of "Missouri white-mule." Especially worthy of note is the characteristic action of the shoulder and right arm in the act of pouring. In these artless delineations of the subtleties of action Bingham shows a constant mastery.

The receiver of the drink (Figure No. 30) is open-mouthed in happy anticipation of his refreshment. He leans back comfortably in the wicker seat, left hand buried in his trousers pocket, the other reaching the glass to the mouth of the jug. The hand with the container is a fluent translation and relation of refined values. The figure in the painting which was based upon this sketch is slightly adjusted to make way for the bare foot of the playing child seated upon the ground (Figure No. 31).

As Bingham has written below (the only comment the artist wrote upon any of these drawings), this is a drawing of Horace Bingham, his oldest son and the constant playmate of the oldest brother of Mr. C. B. Rollins.[57] The lad is engrossed in a game of mumblety-peg. In the painting the boy is shown to be dressed in a manner more appropriate to the occasion. He wears a coat instead of the jacket which is drawn in the sketch. This notation was evidently made quickly.

Directly behind the aforementioned drinker is the figure of a rather poorly garbed individual (Figure No. 32) who seems to be rushing forward to be of assistance in holding up a fellow voter who has drunk well but not too wisely. The action represented here is excellent, for the man seems to be moving to extend a helping hand. Incidentally, in many of the Renaissance masters' sketches, the foreshortening of arms and fingers is not handled with much greater exactness and ease than that with which Bingham renders it in this drawing.

The helpful but distressed citizen supporting the sagging figure of a companion (Figure No. 33) who will probably not vote today, gave Bingham some difficulty. There are two preliminary drawings for these figures, and it seems that the artist took parts of one with the best sections of the other to complete his idea within the painting. It may be, the pose being difficult for the model, that he was hurried to make quick notations, and, not satisfied with one attempt, he reanalyzed his subjects. It is remarkable that the inebriated character gives such a complete characterization of a man abjectly drunk.

Figure No. 33 is undoubtedly the first and less satisfactory sketch, not the one adopted by Bingham for use in his finished work. However, it will be seen that, had he painted the supporting figure with face turned to his right, the composition would have been broken into scenes of major interest with a dividing line between the two. Employing the sound compositional theory that the direction to which the eye is pointed creates a connecting line between the eye and object, Bingham nicely avoids the danger of splitting his composition. He uses the head of the background figure of the first sketch and applies it to his second. The brush work in the former is not as good as Bingham usually attains.

We can recognize the position of the next figure (Figure No. 34) only by the head and characteristics of the face. In the painting, this figure is nearly obliterated by the man immediately in front of him. This sketch is an inimitable caricature of a wizened, elderly, little person, hands folded behind him, belly protruding to an astonishing degree, and head tipped in an attitude of entertained attention. His toothless mouth, with withered gums, is clamped between a Hapsburg chin and a sharp Roman nose. From some viewpoints this is one of the best caricatures Bingham has recorded.

Two figures engaged in animated discussion (Figure No. 35) are also incorporated into the second plane of the painting. Though in the canvas they are reduced to a very low value, being just back of the penetrating light area which distinctly binds the figures in the first plane, they are, in the sketch, exactly drawn in strong black and white. The speaking partner is evidently bringing home to his listeners a salient point to clarify an obtuse phrase in some political issue. His eyes are afire with enthusiastic conviction and his face earnestly beseeches a unanimity of opinion. With pointed forefinger he counts off the number of his postulates upon the digits of his left hand.

What makes Bingham's sketched observations so revealing is the fact that he managed to accumulate such a wide variety of facts which may be said to be typical of man's most frequently employed and telltale gestures, actions, facial expressions and body postures. For example, the man being subjected to the stern "logic" is, though his back is turned to us, obviously listening, but not willingly supporting his instructor's theses. This is somehow indicated by the stubborn, backward swing of the shoulders. The folds of the coat on this figure are economically modeled with form-tracing, cross-hatched lines.

On the far end of the steps a senile old man is tottering down. The drawing (Figure No. 36) is a beautifully executed interpretation of character. With fluent line and strong black and white variations the artist has depicted a remarkable personage.

Seated upon the second step of the stairway is the figure of a man writing his choice of candidates upon note paper or recording the votes for his private satisfaction as the voters call out their man from the top of the platform (Figure No. 37). The sketch shows this man absorbed in his scribblings, making his notes upon the sheet of paper held on his right knee. Later Bingham decided that the figure would seem more natural if the left leg were crossed over the right, thus giving a slightly higher support to the paper. This incident discloses the thoroughness and long-contemplated analysis which Bingham expended upon even seemingly insignificant problems.

A friend is leaning over the shoulder of the seated figure and reading very seriously from the page (Figure No. 38). This figure is exactly reproduced in the painting, except for an alteration in the value of the vest and trousers. In the painting the white shirt is a necessary device to set the man off from a dark foreground portion.

As excellent as were Bingham's efforts with the brush, he did not always reach the height that he achieved in recording the action of two intense and somber citizens engaged in conversation (Figure No. 39). The tilt of the head on the shoulders of the elderly man, who is listening with apparent incredulity to the message of his informer, is a masterpiece of drawing. Cane in hand, and arm akimbo, he expresses wordlessly his captivating robustness of character. The brush work in this phase of the drawing is lucid and illustrative. When studying this sketch, the observer may note that Daumier's lithographs, depicting his fellow human beings in France at this time, were drawn with a hand that was not more accurate or revealing than was Bingham's in this example.

There is another citizen (Figure No. 40) standing close by, who also hears the discourse of the speaker just referred to. A farmer who has come to speak his vote is standing with hands under his coat-tails, scowling in concentration upon the words he hears. This figure is solidly drawn, the pull of the form-filled garments causing wrinkles which are cross-hatched with delightful precision and simplicity.

The figure seated on the barrel (Figure No. 41) is probably not sleeping; the negro freedman has poured too many glassfuls for him and he droops with the stupor of drunkenness. In the painting this figure has been changed a good deal to fit the composition. It is turned slightly more to the three-quarter view instead of profile. His hat has fallen upon the ground and a handkerchief is tied around his throbbing head. Comparing the two figures, however, one can have small doubt that the sketch is the original from which Bingham derived and completed his painted form. In this, as in all of the sketches, Bingham has noted carefully all the minutest differences in the shape of the shoes. In so many of the drawings the boots alone are sufficient to give a clue as to the profession of the character.[58]

The final drawing that we have, which is obviously a preliminary study for *County Election*, is the seated man reading a newspaper. This drawing has been merely the tentative suggestion to the artist and not well done, from which he has developed the figure within the painting. The drawing shows a bumpkin reading avidly and with some humor a notice in the newspaper. His boots, with trousers folded inside, indicate that he is not a city dweller but probably a farm hand from the surrounding territory. The values are quite dark with a few high lights running along the right arm and leg. The painting shows us a better turned-out gentleman, one that Bingham probably assumed would be more likely to read a newspaper at this assembly. This is the figure with the gray top hat, located on the extreme right side of the canvas.

Canvassing for a Vote

The *Candidate Electioneering*, spoken of as the second painting in Bingham's studio in October, is no doubt the canvas we know as *Canvassing for a Vote*. There is only a lithograph to show us what was the nature of this picture,[59] but there is no question that this engraving was made rather exactly from the painting because the sketches are so identical with the figures of the engraving. A writer in the *New York Mirror*, September, 1852, describes the painting as "a small cabinet piece of some four or five figures, forming an out-of-door group, which is composed of the candidate or his friend electioneering for him, endeavoring to circumvent an honest old countryman, who has by his side a shrewd old fellow, who cannot be readily taken in." [60] The picture must have been rather dark, containing four figures, three of them in various attitudes of reaction to the canvasser, who is no doubt speaking for himself or for a friend. The inevitable dog is again in this picture.[61] The structure in the background is said to have been a building in Bingham's home town, Arrow Rock.[62]

The enthusiastic solicitor (Figure No. 42) is seated upon a chair, leaning forward with the intensity of his pronouncements. The drawing is said by some to be a portrait of Bingham himself, but this is probably not so, because the face is not that of the artist.[63] The canvasser is dressed for travel, evidently making the rounds on his horse, soliciting all his friends, trying to influence them as to whom they should favor with their ballot. The sketch itself is nearly a completed portrait. The face is done in cast-drawing detail.

Skeptically listening to his arguments is the prosperous-looking gentleman (Figure No. 43), probably a guest in the tavern. He leans back comfortably in his chair, right hand jammed into his trousers pocket, and his left fingering his cane, which has been drawn in over the folds of the trousers. The figure in the engraving lacks some of the definiteness of the sketch itself, and we could wish to see in actuality the original painting which was based upon the drawings.

COUNTY ELECTION

PLATE VII

The last two paintings discussed by the visitor to Bingham's studio in October, *Chess Players* and a *Landscape Scene on the Ohio*, were not described and have not since been uncovered.

From St. Louis on November 24, 1851, Bingham wrote to his Columbia friend signifying that he and his wife planned to remain in the metropolis throughout the winter and that his employment would be largely the painting of portraits.

"I am more fully confirmed since I came here in the opinion which I expressed to you of the propriety of a full and open expression throughout the state, of the Whig sentiment upon the slavery question. The differences of opinion that really exist, will then be clearly seen, and certain *politicians* may be able to discover that an abstraction may prove a two-edged sword and be as potent in keeping men out of office as in placing them in. . . .

"My better half, whom you were pleased to rate a little lower than the best half of yourself, reached me safely on last Tuesday evening, and we are now fortunately provided with comfortable quarters for the winter. I have been engaged in painting portraits since I came down, and perhaps will be so employed during the greater part of the winter. . . ."

There is a painting, *Belated Wayfarers*, which Bingham may have executed about this time. McCaughen and Burr, St. Louis owners of the painting, attribute it to him because, as in the case of their other picture, *Captured by Indians*, it is signed and dated. The owners evidently have no reliable history of the painting. Miss May Simonds in an article entitled "A Pioneer Painter," contained in the *American Illustrated Methodist Magazine*,[64] remembers two pictures named *White Women Stolen by Indians* and *Emigrants Resting at Night*. She describes these compositions as "night scenes with campfires." She presumably is referring to the McCaughen and Burr paintings. Just where she obtained her information about these pictures is not known.

An examination of *Belated Wayfarers* reveals two figures, one lying asleep upon the ground. The other, an older man, is dozing, although he was evidently assigned to keep watch. He is in a sitting position. Light from the campfire penetrates into the composition from the right side. Two horses are faintly discernible in the background on the left. The

[71]

rump of one and the head of the other form a lighter pattern against the blackness of the night. The composition is arranged in a manner strange to the design usually found in a Bingham work. It seems to lack the studied care which the artist exerted upon his arrangements. The drawing, however, is more Binghamesque than the representation in *Captured by Indians*. The seated figure, especially, is done in a drawing style which might conceivably have been done by the hand of our artist. However, the canvas can by no means be taken as a typical work by Bingham. More evidence is required to establish its authenticity.

Early in June, 1852, Bingham spent perhaps a fortnight in Baltimore as a delegate to the Whig convention. The end of the month found him in Philadelphia making arrangements for the engraving of *County Election*. John Sartain was finally given the commission.[65]

"Philadelphia June 27, 1852

". . . I have fixed my headquarters in this city for one month, and have had an interview with two of the most eminent (engravers) here in relation to my County Election.

"They seem to be delighted with the picture and express a strong desire to be employed to engrave it. One of them, Mr. Sartain, (of Sartain's Magazine), made me a proposition which after hearing from all others I may conclude to accept. He is very ambitious, and his anxiety to add to his already extended reputation by engraving such a work, has induced him to propose terms far below what I anticipated, and which he says will merely enable him to live while the work is in progress. He agrees to finish the plate in his best style of line and Mezzotint for $2,000, $1,200 to be paid in installments as the work proceeds, and the balance from the first funds realized from the subscriptions. He has long had the reputation of being the best Mezzotint engraver in the union, and engraves very well in line also, of which I was not aware until recently.

"One of the prints of the American Art Union of New York is from his hand, and also one of the best prints published by the Philadelphia Art Union.

"If employed upon my work, he promises to devote himself to it exclusively, and expresses confidence in being able to produce a picture superior to any that has yet been published in the United States. His connection with the Magazine would also enable him to have it placed under favorable auspices before the public. Upon the whole, as at present advised, I am strongly disposed to listen to his proposition, but will do nothing hastily. Let me have your advice. Should I close with his offer, I shall be compelled to look to your kindness to procure me the twelve hundred dollars to be paid in the installments as required, and will willingly mortgage to you as security my property at Arrow Rock.

"Mr. Sartain tells me, that by giving his exclusive attention to the work, he can complete it in 15 or 18 months, this will enable me to realize funds from the subscription much sooner than I expected.

"My picture of the 'Raftsmen at Cards,' published by Goupil and Co., and *Dedicated to Major J. S. Rollins of Missouri,*' is now out, and is far superior to the 'Jolly Flat-boatmen.' I have reserved a fine proof copy for you. Remember me to Mrs. R. and the children.

"Sincerely Yours

"G. C. Bingham."

Written on the side is the following:

"The low price at which Mr. Sartain proposes to engrave my picture, I wish to be kept from the knowledge of the public. $4,000 he says he would charge at the rate he is paid for other works, but will engage upon mine as a work of love."

After being exhibited in Columbia, *County Election* was finally sold to Robert J. Ward of Louisville, Kentucky, for $1,000, with the reservation that it should later be exhibited in various cities, and, further, that Sartain might finish his work in making the engraving of it.[66]

Bingham, according to a letter which has no particular interest other than a personal one for his friend, indicated that he was in St. Louis on January 24, 1853, and planned to remain there until spring.

". . . I shall remain here until the first of March, provided I find employment sufficient to make my stay profitable.

"It will take me about two weeks yet to complete my present engagements. . . ."

A letter written on March 9, 1853, contains the information that he will leave for New Orleans, where he plans to lecture (but never does) and that he is fairly prosperous.

". . . I have at length completed my engagements in this city and will embark for New Orleans tomorrow morning.

"I have taken into consideration your advice in reference to lectures on art as a means of facilitating subscriptions to the 'County Election,' and have concluded to test my powers in *that line* upon the occurrence of a favorable opportunity.

"I have had a very close winter's work, and find myself just $500, the better by it clear of all expenses. Three hundred dollars of this sum I can spare for Sartain, and wish you to notify me when he draws upon you so that I may, to that amount at least, contribute to fill the order. I expect to be in New Orleans or vicinity at least six weeks. . . ."

From letters dated May 22 and July 5 and sent from Lexington, Kentucky, we gather that the artist has been on a tour with the painting *County Election*, securing subscribers for copies of the engraving which were to be printed in the summer of 1854.

". . . While my picture remained in Louisville the press was profuse in its commendations, and without a dissenting voice it was pronounced superior to anything of the kind which had yet been seen in America. In reference to the use of it this summer Mr. Ward came fully up to the expectations which I had been led to indulge, and in other respects bestowed every attention calculated to advance my wishes.

"I arrived in this city day before yesterday, and last evening succeeded in placing the 'County Election' where it can be favorably seen tomorrow, which will be Monday.

"I obtained thirty five subscribers in Louisville, not more than half the number that doubtless would have subscribed had my subscription book been presented at the first exhibition of the picture. . . ."

". . . As to the success of my enterprise, it may perhaps be regarded fully equal to what I have a right to expect. I have visited the principal towns in the vicinity of Lexington only and have added to my list about one hundred and fifty subscribers since I came to the state, of the best and most reliable class of citizens. I was in Danville last week, and secured there a liberal subscription considering the population of the place. . . . I find you still insisting upon the lectures. I can but confess my delinquency in suffering my inconvenient modesty thus far to keep the upper hand of your very kind advice. I have really, however, found no occasion since I have been in the state, on which I thought an address upon art would prove available.

"At Danville the weather was so unsufferably hot as to render it painful to listen to even eloquent speakers, and I do not know but an attempted speech from me would have been voted a bore.

[74]

COUNTY ELECTION

PLATE VIII   OWNED BY ST. LOUIS MERCANTILE LIBRARY

NO. I

COUNTY ELECTION

PLATE VIII

NO. 2   ENGRAVING

"My experience so far leads me to believe that what would be calculated to secure success in many undertakings has but little influence in behalf of the interest in which I have embarked. On court days and public occasions generally, large crowds gather around my picture, but no 'material aid' is furnished. And it is only when three or four can contemplate it without interruption that the bait is taken. . . .

"Soon after I came to Kentucky I wrote to Mr. Sartain and afterwards received a letter in reply. . . . He was still progressing satisfactorily with the plate, but did not have it sufficiently advanced to send a proof. When he has it further advanced, he says his calls upon us will be more frequent. . . ."

October 3, 1853, finds Bingham in Philadelphia, supervising the work of the engraving.

". . . The County Election appears to me to be progressing rather slowly, tho' Mr. Sartain assures that it will be completed by the 20th December, which is the time specified in the contract. He appears to be taking a great deal of care in the execution of the work, making the *line* greatly preponderate over the *Mezzotint*. This line process is very slow and tedious, but it marks a picture so deeply into the plate that almost any number of impressions can be made from it. Mr. Sartain tells me that the plate of the County Election, in the manner he is completing it, will make eighteen or twenty thousand good prints.

"I visited New York a few days since. The crystal palace appears to have attracted thither a great many strangers. Having but little time, I passed hurriedly thru the exhibition. I saw a few good pictures and several fine productions of the chisel. I called upon the two houses which are engaged most extensively in the picture trade, Goupil and Co. and Williams and Stevens. Goupil expressed regret that his agent had not contracted with me to publish the County Election. He proposed a partnership with me in the print, after my subscribers shall have been supplied, he to pay half the cost of the plate, etc. and receive half the profits arising from the sale. Such might perhaps turn out to be a good arrangement for me as the house has the command of a very extensive market.

"Williams and Stevens told me they would like much to have the sale of the engravings, and that they would make me a proposition in reference to it shortly. I shall take time to consider well before making any definite arrangement with either house.

"Goupil is anxious to publish another superior and more costly engraving from the Emigration of Boone provided he can obtain upon reasonable terms the use of the picture for that purpose. As the raffle has not yet taken place, we know not into whose hands it may fall. I presume, however, that the owner, whoever he may be, would be willing to part with it for a few months. . . ."

County Canvass or *Stump Speaking*

On November 7 Bingham corresponds with his lawyer friend, informing him of the fact that he has begun his *County Canvas* (Plate IX).

"Philadelphia, Nov. 7, 1853
". . . As your knowledge of my habits may lead you to suppose, I have not been idle during my sojourn here, I am very busily engaged upon my companion to the 'County Election'—the 'County Canvass.' I have already completed the drawing and am proceeding rapidly with the painting. As much as you admired the 'County Election,' I think you will be still better pleased with the present work. I have found less difficulty in the management of the subject, admitting as it does of a much greater variety of attitude, if not of expression. Sartain is very much pleased with the drawing and the grouping of the figures, and surrenders the opinion which he had previously entertained that I would not be able to surpass the 'County Election.' . . .

"I expect to have my 'County Canvas' ready for exhibition by the time Sartain terminates his labors upon the Election, and be obtaining subscribers for *that* while distributing the print of the other. . . ." [67]

That Bingham is by now very confident of his success in the field of genre painting and also that his work is being favorably received is indicated in the letter dated November 23, 1853, and sent from Philadelphia.

". . . Mr. Sartain assures me that the plate will be completed about the time specified in the contract. . . . So far as I am able to determine without a proof, he is executing his work in a superb and masterly manner, and I have a strong hope that he will realize his expectations in the production of the best print that has yet been published on this side of the Atlantic. . . .

"From the recent elections in New York, and other equally significant indications, I am inclined to think our democratic president will not be permitted to sleep very soundly this winter. . . . It will be a glorious time for the country when the present party organizations shall be broken up entirely. We need not expect until then to have a revival of the good old times, when honesty and capacity, rather than party servility, will be the qualifications for office. But I forget that I am a painter and not a politician. I am getting along, fully up to my expectations upon the 'County Canvass,' and flatter myself that I will have it nearly finished by the beginning of the new year. I should like much for you to see it in its present state. I do not think you would counsel any change in the design, and if you did, I scarcely think your advice would be followed. The fact is I am getting to be quite conceited, whispering sometimes to myself, that in the familiar line which I have chosen, I am the greatest among all the disciples of the brush, which my native land has yet produced. When I get this picture completed, and published in conjunction with the 'County Election,' I think I shall have laid the foundation of a fortune sufficient to meet my humble expectations, and place my little family beyond the reach of want, should I be taken away from them. I expect to return to Missouri as soon as my engraving is printed, as the first distribution is to be made there. . . ."

Bingham is reported to have said that he never consciously painted into these political scenes any portraits of known individuals, that the figures were composites drawn from his imagination. Two of Bingham's letters to Rollins, however, seem to indicate that he did portray his acquaintances. C. B. Rollins says, "I have seen so-called keys to Bingham's Election Series purporting to identify with local characters many of the figures in the pictures."[68] Such keys were not without reason, apparently, and must have created great entertainment.

That the interest to identify some of the figures in the painting has not waned even to this day is shown by the fact that the writer received several letters from persons whose ancestors, they claimed, were portrayed here.

When *Life* magazine displayed some of the paintings and drawings of this volume, in the issue of September 11, 1939, such interest was again renewed. One of the most interesting letters came from Miss Ginger Rogers, Hollywood actress, who states that many of the prominent figures in this painting, *Stump Speaking*, are her relatives.

". . . I have quite a serious notion to follow your suggestion and make *Old Bullion appealing to the people of Missouri* the subject of a future picture. That passage in the commencement of his speech at Fayette, in which he designates the friends he came to address, as those only who had *heads to perceive and hearts to feel the truth*, would afford, I think, the best point of time for pictorial representation, as the action which accompanied it, and gave it such emphasis, would display his fine portly figure to the best advantage, and also tell with most happy effect in the faces of the audience. The subject possesses additional recommendation to me, from the fact, that I could introduce in it the portraits of many of my friends who were present upon the occasion, and by a license, which painters, as well as poets can take, I could make others present in the picture who were not present in fact. I think an engraving from such a work would sell, and if painted on a large scale it would be well suited for a place either in the capitol or university of our state. . . ." [69]

> "Philadelphia
> "December 12, 1853

". . . My 'County Canvass' will keep me, I think, fully employed until the Election is ready for distribution. *The Gathering of the Sovereigns* is much larger than I had counted upon. A new head is continually popping up and demanding a place in the crowd, and as I am a thorough Democrat, it gives me pleasure to accomodate them all. The consequence of this impertinance on side, and indulgence on the other, is, that instead of the select company which my plan at first embrased, I have an audience that would be no discredit to the most populous precinct of Buncombe.

"I have located the assemblage in the vicinity of a mill, Kit Bullards perhaps. The cider barrel being already appropriated in the Election. I have placed in lieu thereof, but in the background, a watermellon wagon over which a darkie, of course presides. This waggon and the group in and around looming up in the shadow, and relieved by the clear sky beyond, forms quite a conspicuous feature in the composition, without detracting in the slightest degree from the interest inspired by the principal group in front.

"In my orator (Figure No. 47) I have endeavored to personify a wiry politician grown gray in the pursuit of office and the service of party. His influence upon the crowd is quite manifest, but I have placed behind him a shrewd clear-headed opponent who is busy taking notes, and who will, when his turn comes make sophisms fly like cobwebs before the housekeepers broom (Figure No. 46). . . .

"The public must begin to perceive by this time that our 'new president Pierce' has really nothing in him. Although I gave but 3 cents for his message, I soon discovered that I was badly cheated. . . ."

STUMP SPEAKING

PLATE IX

The painting to which Bingham had reference in the last letter is now known by the name *Stump Speaking* (Plate IX). It is on a canvas 42½ x 58, signed 1854, and owned by the St. Louis Mercantile Library. It represents vividly a most absorbing scene: a political speaker, with experienced force, holds the audience in rapt attention. Dozens of intriguing incidental scenes tantalize the imagination and inevitably force the observer to inspect minutely each square inch to discover another side show.

A careful scrutiny of the canvas will reveal that there are at least seven planes constituting this composition. In the immediate foreground, partially thrown into deep shadow of the first plane, are five figures and two dogs. The initial plane acts as a preliminary screen.[70] It may be compared somewhat to the apron of a stage. From this point the artist, by contrast in size, depth of value, and brilliancy of hue, throws back the farther light planes.

The second plane is marked by a light stream illuminating a few boys at play. The third is a plane in shadow, a neat technical device to prevent confusion between planes one and three, for in this way the artist obtained adequately strong contrasts. Plane four is again in the sunlight. All the figures in it are marked distinctly against the darker background of the fifth area, in which we see the watermelon wagon. Back of that is the barn, partially in sunlight, and last, the distant expanse of graduated hills. The sky is treated simply in areas of light variations against which is set strongly the massive foreground trees located in the left-hand upper corner.

The speaker dominates by his height and by the brilliance of the light value of his coat against the dark depths of the foliage. He, in turn, is balanced in verticality by the barn in the background.

Seated conspicuously upon the platform is the rotund form of a personage said by Mr. C. B. Rollins to be the image of the Honorable M. M. Marmaduke, a former governor of Missouri (Figure No. 44). "Marmaduke," remembers Mr. Rollins, "was so insulted when even his friends recognized him as this figure that he threatened a libel suit and went so far as to challenge Bingham to a duel." Had the two come to sword points the portly politician would have been greatly handicapped; his expanse would have presented a target impossible to miss with a thrust, no matter how wild.

The graying statesman is looking with calculating eye at the speaker. With lower jaw grimly protruding and folds of flesh cascading down each side of the close-pressed lips, he somewhat resembles a ludicrous bulldog. The massive, leonine head with its mane of coarse, grayed hair must have made the governor an unforgettable sight. Cane in hand, hands resting upon thighs, the guest of honor has given the artist opportunity to perfect another excellent characterization.

Perhaps the most powerful sketch that is contained in the sketchbook is the figure of a listener (Figure No. 45) occupying only a minor place in this composition. He is seated directly below the elephantine figure of the ex-state official and with side-turned head is glancing upward to see the gestures of the speaker. The foreshortening of the facial features has been easily accomplished by the artist. Executed in bold, swift brush lines and laid on strongly with a grayed wash, the sketch is a testimonial of Bingham's brush dexterity. The hands of this man, it will be noted, are drawn in a slightly different fashion than the artist usually employs. These hands are gnarled, workaday hands, the one clenched upon his leg, the other hanging crooked-fingered and relaxed. The spontaneity and looseness of some of the line quality is a joy to any draughtsman's heart.

A figure that was taken by some people to be Bingham himself is seated directly behind the speaker. Though this was probably not meant by the artist to be a self-portrait, it unquestionably is the figure of the opponent "taking notes on his rival's speech and eagerly awaiting to answer him in rebuttal." [71] This scowling figure (Figure No. 46) is ferociously indignant, apparently, over certain false statements that the first speaker has made and is jotting them fiercely upon notebook paper. The sketch is rather lightly done, with legs and feet barely outlined with pencil. Light gray wash was laid over shaded areas. However sketchy, this illustration is a charming example of Bingham's brush work.

The speaker (Figure No. 47), whom Bingham himself has described in his letter to Major Rollins, is in fiery fashion swaying his large audience with that type of oratory which, sadly enough, is no longer employed by our more urbane politicians. The face, topped by a crop of unmanageable hair, reminds one somewhat of some of the portraits of Andrew Jackson. Eyes popping, he is the personification of dramatic power. The lower part of the figure has been loosely drawn in with pencil and shaded with swift parallel strokes. Apparently there was much speculation at the time this picture was exhibited whether this man represented Mr. E. D. Sappington, the former political rival of Bingham. "It makes, of course, an entertaining story but there probably is no basis for it." [72]

Sitting reflectively in the shadow cast by the speaker's platform is the form of a dignified patriarch (Figure No. 48), who is much more convincing in the sketch than in the canvas. Fingers interlaced, with thumbs thoughtfully pressed together, he appears to be listening to a more distant voice. The tired, old face, with eyelids drooping over drowsy eyes, makes of this sketched figure a fine characterization. Again, it seems unfortunate that Bingham did not hold more exactly to his sketches when he painted his canvases.

Seated next to the aforementioned gentleman is a stoop-shouldered grandfather (Figure No. 49), with chin resting upon the end of his stick. He is either completely absorbed with the words flowing from above or he may be watching the dog haunched by his feet. Even the hands of this aged citizen indicate his many years.

Certainly not attending the convention with a conscience to fulfill his duties as a citizen of the commonwealth is the sly-faced scoundrel smirking up at the platform (Figure No. 50). This rascally fellow has come to join disreputable companions and to mingle with the crowd. Most of the citizens are above his station in life. "But this is one time," he seems to be thinking, "when my vote counts as much as that of Marmaduke." Sadly battered hat cocked upon his untended hair, whiskers outlining a droll face, he represents the acme of excellent caricature. The drawing is done in grayish tones.

Sitting low upon the ground in the deep shadow is another form not exactly to be classed with the aristocracy. In posture of body this man, in the sketch, almost corresponds with the figure in the painting. The arms indicate that it is the same man. The head has been turned in the direction of the orator. In the sketch the face is dark with beard, the lips are compressed over the stem of a homemade pipe, and the eyes are vacantly staring. In the background the artist has cross-hatched freely, with a brush, a screen to create contrast for the lighter hat and coat.

Smiling approvingly at the politician and seated just back of the previously described man is a citizen of unquestionable responsibility (Figure No. 51). Jovial, fat, and elderly, he seems to be a type of prosperous landowner. The sketched face is modeled simply but reveals that Bingham knew the fundamentals of the physiognomy and could suggest much with a minimum of effort. The drawing of the hand toying with the cane is a good example of this simple brush treatment.

Directly before this immense gentleman is a fulsome-faced yokel laughing up into the sunlight. In the painting this figure has a hat upon his head. The sketch shows him bareheaded, with a hedge of whiskers along the base of the jaw. A drawing, probably made tentatively, is not as surely developed in all parts as Bingham usually draws his sketches. The right hand and the left boot, however, are minutely analyzed. The most interesting portion of this plate is the sketch of the foreshortened arm and hand in the right-hand upper corner. Little touches like this one would substantiate Arthur Pope's argument that Bingham was truly a Renaissance remnant.

White-suited, top-hatted, and easily the outstanding citizen of the congregation is the gentleman placed in the right of the composition (Figure No. 52). The sketch shows a lean-faced, dignified man, conscious of authority, sitting erectly and concentrating profoundly upon the candidate's message. The artist has written notes concerning color for future reference upon the vest lapel and upon the trouser leg. The excellence of this drawing is self-evident. Bingham inserted this figure knowingly into the right area of the painting to counterbalance the interest contained in the extreme left.

It is surprising to notice the unending effort in thought which Bingham spent over these genre paintings. One can readily believe that he worked assiduously for months to attain that degree of perfection which he demanded in his compositions.

Last and on the extreme right, farthest from the speaker's platform, sits a rustic member of the assembly, intent upon hearing (Figure No. 53). This figure, fully sketched, was but partially shown in the actual painting. The drawing is, nevertheless, executed with painstaking care. The left arm, especially, is worthy of study. It is well formed and suggests realistically the fleshy arm contained in the sleeve. The folds of the top coat, too, are done with commendable care and scholarly simplicity.

It is unfortunate that dozens of figures in the painting are not made more accessible to the critic interested in minutiae, but the sketches were either not made or, more likely, were lost during Bingham's many travels.

On February 1, 1854, Bingham writes from Philadelphia. Evidently he was quite incensed with Sartain's procrastination in engraving *County Election*.

". . . There is a singularity about engravers, from which I find that Mr. Sartain is not exempt. They invariably promise work in less time than it can possibly be performed. . . .

"I am now giving the last touches to my 'County Canvass.' It will be a more imposing and effective picture than the Election, the figures are larger, more varied in character, and also much greater in number. Mr. Sartain thinks that its exhibition will produce quite a sensation here. I wish to take it West with me as soon as my engraving is ready for distribution, which will be in March April or May, as definitely as I can promise myself. . . ."

On April 6 there is another letter from the same location referring to the progress of the engraving and reporting the sale of *County Canvass* to Goupil and Company, who will make an engraving of it.

". . . I am yet watching the 'County Election' in the hands of Mr. Sartain, and am determined to have a satisfactory result, whatever time or labor it may require. . . .

"I sold the copy right of my new picture 'The County Canvass' a few days since to Messrs. Goupil & Co. upon terms perhaps as favourable as any artist ever obtained from a publisher. It will be engraved in Paris in the most superior style. The prints will correspond, in size and in price, with those of the County Election. . . . Since I completed the 'County Canvass' I have painted two small pictures [73] which I sold for three hundred and twenty five dollars, and I shall continue to make the best use of my time as long as I shall be detained here. . . .

"I have already commenced thinking for another large composition, which I will entitle 'The Verdict of the People.' I intend it to be a representation of the scene that takes place at the close of an exciting political contest, just when the final result of the ballot is proclaimed from the stand of the judges. The subject will doubtless strike you as one well calculated to furnish that contrast and variety of expression which confers the chief value upon pictures of this class. I might very properly introduce into it some of those comically long faces which were seen about Fayette . . . last summer. . . ."

The last paragraph of this letter is the first evidence that is recorded giving information concerning the popular *Verdict of the People*. Another letter mentions it again along with the plate for *County Election*.

"New York, May 17, 1854

". . . The plate now appears to be nearly finished, and is coming out much to the satisfaction of the Artists who have seen it. There are a great many small touches, however, yet to be given to it, which will require time, and as not more than twelve or fifteen impressions can be taken in day, I fear September will have arrived before I reach my subscribers. They shall be supplied, however, as soon as possible. As quite a number of proofs will be taken before the plate is lettered, I may meet with an opportunity to send you one in advance.

"I expect to return to Philadelphia tomorrow. I have commenced my studies for the 'Verdict of the People.' I desire it to 'Cap the Climax.' . . ."

In the letter dated May 29 and sent from Philadelphia Bingham gives a further summary of the financial arrangements made with Goupil concerning the publication of engravings made from the plate Sartain had completed of *County Election*.[74]

". . . I wrote to you about ten days since from New York requesting your advice in reference to Mr. Goupil's most favorable proposition to purchase the copy right and plate of the 'County Election,' giving me one dollar more on each of my subscribers than he had previously offered. As he was about embarking for Paris, I concluded upon consultation with two or three gentlemen here, to accept his terms without waiting until your answer reached me. I will merely restate here that according to the contract

[84]

concluded between us, I can secure $7.33 and one third cts. upon each of my subscribers, and $6.33 and one third upon all prints which I may sell hereafter, and the entire expense of engraving, paper, printing and publishing to be borne by Goupil and Co. I would send you a copy of the contract if it were not for its length. . . .

"I enclose you a couple of bad photographs which will give you an idea of the 'County Canvass.' . . ."

Two other letters from Philadelphia mention the *Verdict of the People*.

"Philadelphia July 15, 1854

". . . 'The Verdict of the People' is still growing under my hand, and I expect to have it sufficiently completed to exhibit to advantage by the time I shall be able to leave. It is much larger, and will combine more striking points than either of its predecessors. . . ."

"Philadelphia Jan. 12, 1855

". . . I had the good fortune to reach the city of brotherly love in good time to share the greetings of the New Year.[75] My return so early was somewhat unexpected, as I deemed it probable that I would be compelled to visit the interior towns of Kentucky in which my subscribers of that state were located; but I effected a sale of my subscription list, and the prints necessary to fill it, with the firm of Hegan Escott & Moose of Louisville, which relieved me from the task of distributing in person and enabled me to return and resume my labors upon the 'Verdict of the People.' I hope to complete this last of the series early in the spring. I have heard from my 'County Canvass' since it reached Paris. It has been committed to the hands of one of the *very best* of the eminent engravers of that city. The name of the engraver is *Gotier*. I have seen several large engravings, of surpassing excellence, from plates executed by him. . . .

"What is the chance for a pictorial embellishment for the Capitol? There is no other edifice, of such magnificence, in the union, which presents such a space of bare walls. If you are not ripe for such a work of art as the Emigration of Boone upon a large scale would be, a full length portrait of Washington might do for a beginning. Were I to receive a commission from the state for such a work I would be ambitious to render it *superior* to that which graces the Hall of Representation at Washington. I should like to present the 'Father of his Country,' connected with some historical incident, in a manner that would rival the far famed picture by Luitze. . . ."

[85]

Bingham probably left Philadelphia in the early spring of 1855. He sends the next letter from Independence, Missouri, June 21, 1855, with the following happy news:

"I completed my picture of the 'Verdict of the People' before I left Philadelphia, and forwarded it to New York where it will await an answer from Goupil (who is now in Paris), in regard to terms of publication. I deemed it best not to have it exhibited in advance. All, however, who had seen it, pronounce it the best of my works. . . .

"I expect to go to Paris this fall, . . . will remain there until the engravings of the County Canvass and Verdict of the People shall be completed. . . ."

Verdict of the People

Today there are extant two paintings depicting this scene of the announcement of election returns. By far the better is the painting from which later an engraving was made. It is owned by the Mercantile Library. The other is owned by Mr. J. W. S. Peters of Kansas City. "The latter is definitely the replica," says Mr. C. B. Rollins.[76] Though the two paintings are similar in a general way (i. e., the masses of the two compositions are identically placed and many of the figures are similar), nevertheless, after close research, numerous discrepancies are apparent.

In the immediate foreground the negro pushing the wheel barrow differs slightly in the two canvases. The announcer of the votes is not the same man in both compositions. And so, as we compare one painting with the other, we detect innumerable small unlikenesses. Perhaps the most obvious point of distinction lies in this: the flag in the Mercantile-owned work is flown from a pole extended from the pillared building on the left of the composition, while in the work owned by Mr. Peters the flag is hung from a line which runs from the aforementioned building to a structure across the street. The St. Louis-owned version of *Verdict of the People* is reproduced here (Plate X). It has been newly restored and is now displayed in the St. Louis City Museum.

"If one were to consider merely the general arrangement of a picture like the *Verdict of the People*, one might say that it was done by some follower of Poussin. . . . One finds a screen of architecture brought

VERDICT OF THE PEOPLE

PLATE X

across the upper left portion to the central vertical axis of the picture, leaving the upper right portion for distant background, in the manner inaugurated by Giorgione, Titian and Palma and continued by Poussin and Claude and other painters of the seventeenth and eighteenth centuries."

Further, ". . . the main mass of figures at the left is brought out in light against a moderately darker background, while the mass of figures on the right is thrown into shadow against light beyond; the central axis is accented by the group slightly separated from the rest of the foreground action and yet belonging to it; one proceeds from large masses down to smaller groups in a perfectly clear and orderly manner. Ability to handle large numbers of figures in this way is one of the rarest things in the history of painting. Some contemporary renderings of the American scene seem rather poverty-stricken in comparison with Bingham's orderly procedure and fertility of invention." [77]

Evidently Bingham did not bother to bring back with him to Missouri the sketches which he unquestionably used in Philadelphia while at work on this painting. There can be no question that he did use models, because when he did not, as in the case of *Order No. 11*, there is a quality lacking in his character conceptions. In the *Verdict of the People* the figures, every one, are represented with that truthfulness and attention to detail which is typical of the characteristics contained in the paintings in which we know he introduced studied forms. The sketches, then, for the *Verdict of the People* were either destroyed or were left in Philadelphia.

The Late Work and Political Life

FROM September, 1855, until the spring of 1856 Bingham was occupied in painting portraits in Columbia and Jefferson City, and by March 14, 1856, he was making his initial studies for his historical *Washington Crossing the Delaware*, a painting upon which the artist labored for almost sixteen years.[1] This canvas is now in the private collection of Mrs. Thomas H. Mastin of Kansas City.[2] Bingham is said to have been inspired by the painting of the same subject executed by Leutze, a contemporary German painter.[3]

The story, so well known to all school children, is here illustrated over-dramatically and unrealistically. The painter, motivated by patriotic emotions, obviously was intending further to immortalize George Washington's name, and he did this with all the power of which he was capable. The hero, seated upon the "spirited white charger," is placed directly in the center of the composition. His cohort surrounds him on every side. In the company are lieutenants on horseback, soldiers with bayoneted guns, and others with oars and pikes to guide the raft through the ice. We feel, in examining this composition, that Bingham for once was "out of his element."

The drawing, however, is solid and professional and the arrangement of the figures is about what one would expect from a man of Bingham's temperament, who was then working from pure imagination. Bingham, like Thomas Benton, another Missourian, cannot rightly be spoken of as a highly imaginative creator. He, like Benton, needs must see the object matter before him.[4]

Writing from Louisville, Kentucky, June 2, 1856, Bingham, after giving vent to a few explosive views on slavery, tells his friend:

". . . I expect we shall go directly to Phil. from this city. from thence I will go to Washington and then to Boston in order to copy heads of Washington and Jefferson for the State picture.

"My 'Verdict of the People' has been highly relished by the people here. I did not open a subscription, but engaged to one house in the city $400 worth of prints to be delivered as soon as published. . . ."

As Bingham predicted, he did arrive in Boston and writes to Major Rollins from there on June 29, 1856.

". . . Although detained beyond my expectations I have not been idle. I copied Stuarts portraits of Washington and Jefferson, and executed private commissions besides, to the amount of four hundred dollars. I found an excellent portrait of Jefferson by Stuart in the possession of ex Gov Coles of Philadelphia, who had purchased it at Mrs. Madison's sale to whose order it was originally painted from life. You are likely somewhat acquainted with the history of Gov. Coles. He was the private Sec. of Mr. Madison, and was subsequently appointed by Pres. Monroe Territorial Gov. of Illinois. He is well acquainted with all the prominent men who figured in the early history of our own *Border Ruffian State*, Barton, Benton, Bates, and others. . . .

"He insisted upon my occupying a room in his house while executing the copy. . . .

"I have completed in this city, the head of Washington from the great original by Stuart which hangs in the gallery of the Boston Athenium.

"Here, too, every facility was afforded me in the accomplishment of my wishes. The president of the institution, Mr. Perkins, not only granted permission to copy, but remove the picture if I should deem it necessary to any position most favorable to my purpose. By using a screen, however, I secured an excellent light, where it hung, and have completed a copy, which has been certified by the President of the Art Commission, the librarian and also by the Mayor of Boston as *excellent and faithful in every particular*. The librarian considered it decidedly the best that had ever been taken. . . ."

Evidently changing his plans, which were probably to sail to Europe from Boston, the artist returns to Philadelphia. On August 10, 1856, he gives an account of his activities to Major Rollins.

". . . Although disappointed in not embarking as early as I expected, I have turned my detention to profitable account. Upon my return from Boston with my copy of Stuarts portraits of Washington & Martha Washington Mr. Earle, the principal picture dealer in this city gave me an order for six copies of the copy, which order I have just completed entirely to his satis-

[89]

faction. He pays me for these copies $380.00. I painted them in less than two weeks time. I have also painted other pictures for different individuals to the amount of $300.00. These sums will be amply sufficient for passages and expenses for some time to come should we reach Paris safely.

"We will leave here on next Wednesday for New York, where we will embark on the Steam Ship *Vigo* direct for Havre. She leaves Aug. 14. . . .

"After I complete the portraits for our State Capitol, I have it in contemplation to paint a new series of pictures illustrative of 'Squatter Sovereignty' as practically exhibited under the workings of the Kansas Nebraska bill. I shall commence with the *March of the 'Border Ruffians,'* and will take pains to give those infamous expeditions of unorganized rowdyism all those odious features which truth and justice shall warrant.

"I will want a portrait of Col Samual Young, of a big negro that played the violin, and of a certain methodist parson. As I desire to give this trio the most conspicuous position upon the canvas, cannot you manage to forward them to me. . . ."

To our great loss Bingham did not carry out this plan. "*The March of the Border Ruffians* was never painted," says Mr. C. B. Rollins.

Arriving in France, the artist pens the following letter from Paris, September 7, 1856:

". . . As you may suppose I employed my earliest leisure in a visit to the gallery of the Louvre. The great collection of works of Art there from all nations and schools perhaps afford a student advantages which he cannot obtain elsewhere. But unless he possessed the power to retain a clear perception of nature through the various guises in which she is here portrayed, like a juror staggering in doubt, scarcely knowing whether he inclined to truth or falsehood. Yet amidst the many conflicting statements presented by the masters of the various schools, there are numerous facts to be found, most forcibly and clearly expressed, which may be laid hold of by a matured judgment and used to great advantage. I shall be compelled to visit the great gallery often before I can be able properly to appreciate the treasures which it contains. . . ."

The artist visits for several months in the city; but becoming discouraged with conditions, he continues on to Düsseldorf where he finds everything to his liking and writes enthusiastically on November 4, 1856.

[90]

FIG. 1

FIG. 2

FIG. 3

FIG. 4

FIG. 5

FIG. 6

FIG. 7

FIG. 8

FIG. 9

FIGURES 1–9

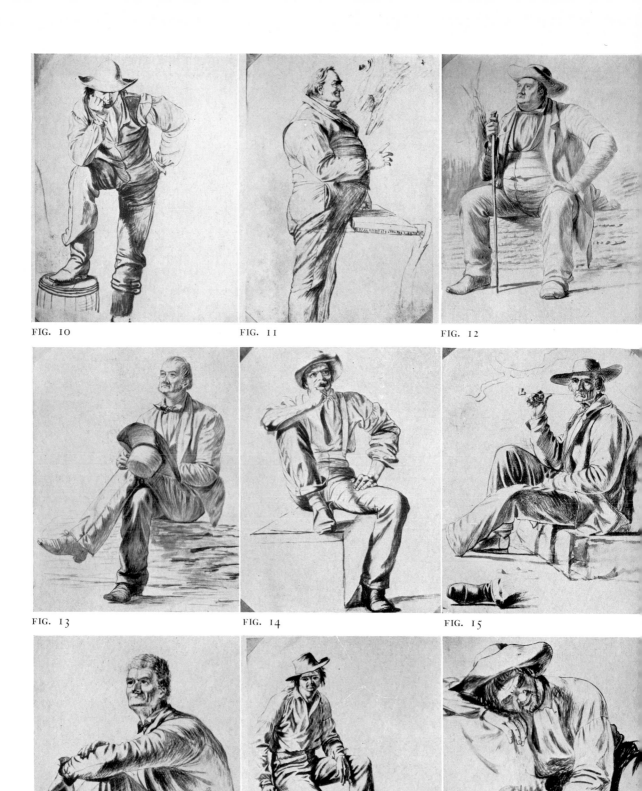

FIG. 10 FIG. 11 FIG. 12

FIG. 13 FIG. 14 FIG. 15

FIG. 16 FIG. 17 FIG. 18

FIGURES 10–18

FIG. 19

FIG. 20

FIG. 21

IG. 22

FIG. 23

FIG. 24

IG. 25

FIG. 26

FIG. 27

FIGURES 19-27

F<small>IGURE</small> 28

FIGURE 29

FIG. 30 FIG. 31 FIG. 32

FIG. 33 FIG. 34 FIG. 35

FIG. 36 FIG. 37 FIG. 38

FIGURES 30–38

FIG. 39   FIG. 40   FIG. 41

FIG. 42   FIG. 43   FIG. 44

FIG. 45   FIG. 46   FIG. 47

FIGURES 39–47

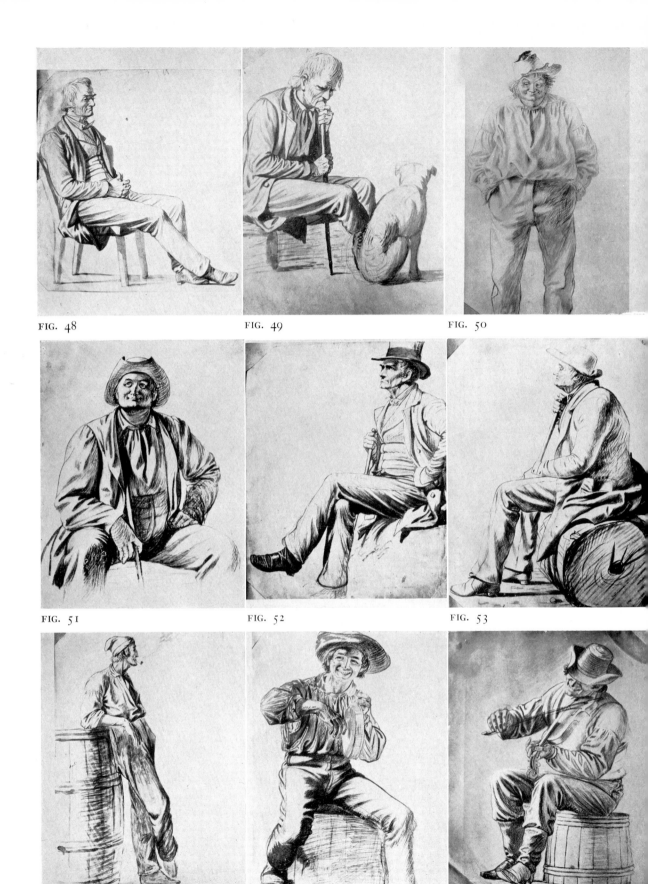

FIG. 48   FIG. 49   FIG. 50

FIG. 51   FIG. 52   FIG. 53

FIG. 54   FIG. 55   FIG. 56

FIGURES 48–56

". . . Dusseldorf is but a village compared with Paris or with our large American cities, yet I question much if there can be found a city in the world where an artist, who sincerely worships Truth and Nature, can find a more congenial atmosphere, or obtain more ready facilities in the prosecution of his studies. . . . I have ordered a large canvass, 8 by 12 feet, for the portrait of Washington, and as soon as it is ready I will commence the work. I have already a small study of the figure which I executed in Paris. I have some idea of painting Jefferson in a sitting posture surrounded by his library and other accessories, indicating his character both as Statesman and Philosopher. Let me have your views in regard to it. I have not yet made any definite arrangements in regard to the publication of my last picture (The Verdict of the People). I made a proposition to Mr. Goupil in Paris who wishes to hear from his agent in New York before responding to it. He informed me that the best engravers in Paris were too much engaged to undertake the work immediately, so that nothing could be lost by a little delay. I was strongly disposed to become my own publisher, and made my terms such as I thought it likely they would reject, and will not be at all dissatisfied should my proposition be declined. . . ."

Having found residence at No. 35 Kaiser Strasse, Düsseldorf, Bingham reports more reasons for his happy state in Prussia. This letter is dated December 14, 1856.

". . . The striking peculiarity of the school which flourishes here by its own inherent vitality, is a total disregard of the 'old masters' and a direct resort to nature for the truths which it employs.[5] As might be expected, works springing from a principle of execution so simple and so rational are characterized by a freshness vigor and truth, which captivates those of common understanding and is none the less agreeable to minds of the highest cultivation.[6] But we will drop the subject of Art for the present, except a single statement, which I must not omit, to the effect that I have the full length of 'The Father of his Country' standing up six feet and a half in my studio, and that the arrangement and general effect of the picture as well as the likeness is highly approved by my fellow-Americans. . . ."

Jolly Flatboatmen

Approximately six months later Bingham imparts some interesting information to Major Rollins. Writing from Düsseldorf, June 3, 1857, he says:

[91]

". . . Soon after we arrived in Dusseldorf I obtained a very comfortable studio for the winter, but after I put up the canvass for the portrait of Washington I perceived that I had not as much space as pictures of such size required. As soon, therefore, as I got it advanced as far, as I deemed it safe to attempt it, towards completion, I postponed it until I could get possession of a large studio, which I succeeded in doing on yesterday. In these my new quarters I have a good light and ample space for pictures of almost any size, and on the same floor with the studio we have our family apartments, which puts us together under the same roof. Liutzes Studio is upon the lot adjoining mine, and as he is the most eminent artist here who speaks English his vicinity is a matter of considerable importance.

"I expect in the course of the summer and fall to complete the portraits both of Washington and Jefferson. I have not determined whether I will send them to you, or keep them until we return home ourselves. This will depend upon the length of time I may deem it our interest to remain here.

"I have made arrangements for publishing the 'Verdict of the People,' and intend to be the exclusive proprietor of the print. . . .

"You ask me if I can make a living by my profession here, I can only reply, that if a painter cannot support himself in Dusseldorf, or any large city in Germany or Italy, he has not merit to entitle him to support anywhere. In order to sell pictures here, however, an artist must employ himself upon European subjects. I have no doubt but I could do well with American subjects by publishing them like the 'Verdict of the People,' and putting them in the American market. I have on hand a large picture of 'Life on the Mississippi' which will not require a great while to complete, and which promises to be far ahead of any work of that class which I have yet undertaken. . . ."

The work which he refers to as *Life on the Mississippi* is the famous genre which has come to be known commonly as *Jolly Flatboatmen* (No. 3). More discussion of this painting is contained in Bingham's next correspondence to his friend, sent from Düsseldorf, October 12, 1857, when he reports that *Jolly Flatboatmen* is nearing completion.

". . . I have made some studies for the portrait of Jefferson, but have not reached a final determination as to the attitude in which I will place him. I think, however, that I will arrive at a conclusion shortly, and set about the execution of the work in earnest. The portrait of Washington receives high praise from all who see it, and I intend to prove that our state is none the loser by employing its own painter. I am now finishing my 'Jolly-flatboatmen

JOLLY FLATBOATMEN

Plate XI
NO. 1

GENERAL LYON AND GENERAL BLAIR

Plate XI
NO. 2

in part,' it is a large picture containing 21 figures. I expect to send you a photograph of it sometime this fall. I have thought of commencing, shortly, my contemplated large picture of the 'emigration of Boone,' 12 by 18 feet, and advancing it in conjunction with the portrait of Jefferson.[7] I think this subject when completed to my mind, united with the two portraits for the State will form a very popular exhibition in the western states especially, and may thus amply repay me for the labor bestowed upon it. I have not yet abandoned my purpose of doing justice in the way of Art, to our *farfamed* 'border ruffians,' and would like you to send me, enclosed in a letter, the most graphic account, extant of one of their most conspicuous forays. . . ."

Revising the idea to which he had given expression over a decade ago,[8] Bingham, thousands of miles removed from his native scene, composed one of his most delightful genre pictures (Plate XI, No. 1). The scene represented reveals a group of happy river men enjoying the antics of a fellow boatman dancing the "hoe-down." [9] As usual Bingham balances the mass of figures dominating one side of the composition with the orthodox device of retreating into the distance in the other portion of the picture. It is true that "the nearer figures seem somewhat artificially placed to keep them from interfering with the main action of the painting," and that "there is a suggestion of amateur acting and stage management" in the conscious arrangement of the figures.[10]

Nevertheless, the picture is not too obviously harmed by these few shortcomings. The frontal plane, consisting of two figures on the extreme left of the composition and including the very foreground thrown into deep shadow, serves as an adequate introduction to the scene of main interest. This group of figures is arranged in pyramidal form but the variations on either side relieve the arrangement from any monotony. The eye of the observer carries across the composition, invited by distance to a secondary scene of interest at which point there are painted two figures concentrating upon an account book. Following this guide, and directed by the structures on the shore line to a passenger boat and the figure of a distant workman, the gaze passes finally into the blurred horizon. The sky is painted in monotone.

The figure most prominent to the left in the foreground is the lanky form of a boatman leaning nonchalantly upon a hogshead (Figure

No. 54). The brush work here is not stroked with Bingham's usual precision, but the sag of the right portion of the torso expresses well the ungainly slouch. It is possible that the artist had a fairly definite visual conception of his composition when he made these sketches, for in the painting this figure is almost a silhouette, while in the sketch those sections which were to be interpreted as one solid mass of dark are drawn with a minimum of detail.

Somewhat similar to the skillet beater (Figure No. 2) represented in the earlier painting of the subject, but with quite different facial expressions, is the sketch of the carefree individual who acts as drummer (Figure No. 55). For some reason Bingham has splashed a few brush lines of opaque onto this drawing. The only reason for this that the writer can discern is that the opaque was once pure white and applied upon the gray-toned paper to effect high lights. Today the drawing has an unpleasant muddy quality. This man seems to be of approximately the same age as the one shown in the Mastin painting.[11] There is some difference in the costume, however.

The preliminary study for the young man with elbow cushioned upon grain sacks is a sketch which varies only in a few minor aspects from the figure in the painting. The back of this youth is turned to us. He is supporting himself with his right arm, the other resting upon his raised left knee. The accurately placed shoulder blades show through the vest. The effect is obtained by the application of neatly cross-hatched brush lines.

The fiddler (Figure No. 56; cf. Figure No. 1) seated on a barrel is enjoying the music, heart and soul. A wide grin spreads across his face as he watches his finger placement upon the neck of his fiddle. With left foot vigorously tapping the tempo, he veritably causes some lively old fiddle tunes to sing in the memory of the observer.

The owner of the flatboat is seen, in the painting, figuring with the shipper the price of transporting the cargo. He is, with tablet held upon his knee, calculating costs very shrewdly, if one may judge by the grim expression on his face.

This *Jolly Flatboatmen*, with the Election Series canvases, all in the possession of the Mercantile Library Association, was exhibited at the

World's Columbian Exposition in Chicago in 1893. This Retrospective Exhibit of American Art contained about a hundred paintings by approximately sixty American artists working during the latter part of the eighteenth and the first half of the nineteenth centuries. "Such artists as Gilbert Stuart, Benjamin West, Washington Allston, John Singleton Copley and Charles W. Peale were represented." [12]

On March 8, 1858, Bingham writes an amusing and entertaining letter to his friend. He is still in Düsseldorf.

". . . I am as closely confined to my studio as ever. I have the portrait of Jefferson now pretty well advanced, and expect to complete it about the first of April. The attitude in which I have placed him, tho erect, is quite different from that given to the portrait of Washington. He stands in the legislative hall with a roll of paper in his left, and a pen in his right hand, and with one foot elevated upon a step of the small platform immediately in front of the speaker's desk. His well-known personal singularity in regard to costume has given me some little advantage. . . . In conversation with his old and intimate friend Gov. Coles, I learned that when he did not wear the scarlet vest he sometimes draped himself in a long light reddish-brown frock coat reaching almost to his ankles, and instead of the then common shoe with the silver buckle he wore an invention of his own which he styled the '*Jefferson* shoe,' and which resembled very closely the present gaiters worn by ladies.

"His object in using so much red in his apparel appears to have been to counteract the effect of a similar hue in his hair. Availing myself of these facts of dress, I am able to make his portrait, in some respects, a complete contrast to that of Washington; and to avoid the repetition in it of anything contained in the latter. I intend it to equal the Washington as a work of Art, and will also be disappointed if both shall not be found to surpass any similar representations of the same personages in any of the states of the union. I have come to the conclusion to forward them to their intended destination during the approaching summer, and I think it perhaps best to have frames made for them here, and forwarded with them, so that they may be put up in their respective places as soon as they reach Jefferson City. . . ."

"Further along in the letter," Mr. C. B. Rollins states, "Bingham says that he can have frames for these portraits made in Düsseldorf much better and more cheaply than in America. In fact, he says that the difference in cost will pay his expenses to Jefferson City, to see that the pictures are properly hung, and back to Düsseldorf. Bingham came from Düsseldorf to Jefferson City in January, 1859, to superintend the hanging of these pictures." [13] Bingham's appreciation of his welcome when he arrived in Jefferson City is contained in a letter written to Rollins from Jefferson City, January 23, 1859.

". . . I am much gratified by the cordiality in which I have been greeted since my return and am consequently cheered by the hope, that my devotion to Art for so many years may at length receive its reward. . . ."

On February 19, 1859, our artist writes from St. Louis.

". . . I feel highly honored by the action of the Legislature upon the reception of the pictures, and in authorizing me, as you have by this time learned, to paint the additional portraits of Jackson and Clay. . . ."

The enthusiasm with which Bingham's commissioned work was received by the people of Missouri is indicated in an article written in the *Jefferson City Inquirer*, entitled "Mr. Bingham's Portrait of Thomas Jefferson." [14]

"This splendid life size painting, by the Missouri Artist, was placed in the Hall of the House of Representatives day before yesterday. It is one of the finest paintings we have ever seen, and will be a lasting monument to the genius and skill of Missouri's Artist . . . Bingham.

"The head of the portrait of Jefferson was copied from the original portrait by Stuart painted for President Madison in the year 1804.

"This original portrait by Stuart is now in possession of Governor Coles of Philadelphia, and was purchased by him at the sale of Mr. Madison's effects, after his decease. Gov. Coles was intimately acquainted with Jefferson, Madison and Monroe, and was appointed, by the latter, Governor of Illinois. He furnished Mr. Bingham with an apartment in his house while Mr. B. was making the copy from which the large picture was painted, and, also, imparted to him valuable information in regard to the costume of the great philosopher and statesman."

The authorization to paint the likeness of Jackson and Clay netted the artist $3,500.

"Probably it was during this short stay in Missouri that he painted the portrait of Dr. Troost of Kansas City." [15] This spontaneous and lifelike portrait of Dr. Troost (Plate XII, No. 1) contains a vitality not always seen in Bingham's portrait work.

In the meantime having received a commission to paint the portrait of Baron von Humboldt for the St. Louis Mercantile Library Association, Bingham set sail for Europe. Arriving in Prussia, our artist writes from Düsseldorf, June 6, 1859:

". . . In the course of ten or twelve days I expect to proceed to Berlin in order to make the necessary studies for the portrait of the Baron von Humbolt. I am assured that there will be no difficulty in finding portraits of him there. I will make an original picture in all except the head and intend to place him in his study—upon his last great work, and surrounded by his favorite authors. The great man left the world on the very day that I reached St. Louis to be honored with a commission to paint his portrait. . . ."

The life-size portrait of the great philosopher and naturalist, Humboldt, hung in the Mercantile Library until, fragile with age, the canvas gave way under the strain of the stretcher. Today the section, a few square feet of canvas, on which is painted the head, is the property of Mr. C. B. Rollins. The paint is laid on very thinly, the pigment dark and dull with accumulated grime.

Bingham's stay in Europe was cut short by the death of Dr. Thomas, his father-in-law. With his family Bingham arrived in New York in September, 1859.

After his return from Europe, Bingham began to work on the Jackson portrait, the head of which was modeled after the famous head by Sully. It was recognized generally as an excellent work of art. "It was a splendid likeness and showed the old warrior dressed in full regimentals astride a spirited charger. The whole was the very incarnation of martial spirited action." [16] In regard to it Bingham writes from Independence, Missouri, September 15, 1860.

". . . I have just completed by far the most difficult work of the two, the equestrian portrait of Jackson and will proceed with the portrait of Clay as soon as I can receive some materials which I have ordered from New York.

"My portrait of Jackson will be pronounced, by connoiseurs and the public, immeasurably superior to any similar work in the United States, the

[97]

great statue at Washington, by Clark Mills, not excepted. The window of my studio commands the main avenue leading from Kansas City towards New Mexico, through which thousands of horses, oxen and mules are almost daily passing, and I have thus had an opportunity for observing by which I have been able to make the charger of the Old Hero as near perfection as possible. The jockeys who attended our County Fair last week will admit that he would have taken the premium from any animal in the ring. But however perfect in symmetry attitude and muscular development the horse may be regarded, the spectator will perceive, at a glance, that the still nobler rider fully maintains his proper preeminence as the chief object of attraction, and that the single spirit of the conqueror of the veterans of Wellington manifests itself in all the subordinate elements of the picture. . . .

"I look forward to the election of Lincoln with far more hope than apprehension, and believe that his administration will allay the present sectional strife by demonstrating to the people of the Southern states that the large majority of their northern brethren are willing to concede to them everything to which they are clearly entitled under the Constitution. . . ."

Then, applying himself to the task of completing the portrait of Clay, Bingham writes to Rollins from Kansas City on November 27, 1860:

". . . Our circumstances at this particular juncture are such as leave me very little leisure. Not being disposed to increase our indebtedness, and being the only member of our household in a condition to earn any money, I have been compelled occasionally to take temporary leave of 'Old Hal' and 'Old Hickory' to provide the wherewithall to feed and clothe us. . . .

"I have been now for some weeks constantly engaged upon my portrait of Clay and expect with good luck to have it completed in about three weeks more. I feel very confident that neither of the portraits will fall behind the expectations of my most sanguine friends. I think they will perhaps surpass both the Washington and Jefferson, as far as they surpass similar works to be found elsewhere in our country. These large works I find better adapted to my powers than the smaller cabinet pictures upon which I had previously been employed. Should I be so fortunate as to get a commission from Congress I have no fear that I will be unable to rival any work which they are likely to obtain from other quarters. I desire to have these portraits at Jefferson at the beginning of the Session of the Legislature, and to fire the Hickory boys by putting up the portrait of Jackson on the eighth of January. . . ."

It was about this time, 1860, that Mr. C. B. Rollins, son of Major James S. Rollins, recollects first seeing George Caleb Bingham.

On January 12, 1861, Bingham writes from Jefferson City:

". . . My Portraits of Clay and Jackson were placed side by side in the Hall of Representatives during the night of the 7th, and from all who loved their country, elicited spontaneous tokens of admiration during the celebration of the 8th. . . ."

This festival was a memorable day, according to the *Jefferson City Inquirer:* [17]

"Celebration of the Eighth of January
"A salute of 33 guns were fired in the morning, and as the sound awoke, the echo on the opposite bluffs, so also did it wake the slumbering population of Jefferson City, who, after due time, wended their way to the Capitol to hear the speeches and see the paintings of Jackson and Clay. The large Hall of Representatives was soon filled with both, strangers and citizens, while some of 'Missouri's fair daughters' lent their beauty and smiles to the occasion. The meeting was called to order by Hon. Thos. A. Harris, of Marion. Loud calls were then made for Geo. C. Bingham, Esq., who came forward, and delivered one of the most Union-loving, and patriotic speeches, that we have ever had the pleasure of hearing. He was frequently and loudly applauded, for his sentiments seemed to be those of the majority of those present. . . .

"The 8th of January may be called 'JACKSON's day,' for he immortalized it by his victory. It was therefore with feelings of unfeigned admiration and pleasure, that the audience contemplated the noble picture of him, by Mr. Bingham. The subject was a fine one, and the artist did it justice. The old hero, is represented as mounted on a charger, waving his hat, and cheering his army on to victory. By the side of this picture, stood one of the immortal orator and statesman—Henry Clay. This is a fine effort, and well sustains the reputation which the artist has already gained. It is worth a visit to the Capitol. Altogether it was a great day, and like the feast of O'Rooke,

"'Twill ne'er be forgot,
By those who were there, and those who were not.'"

The two paintings which were hung that day, as well as the portraits of Washington and Jefferson, were destroyed when the Missouri State Capitol burned in 1911.[18] Mr. C. B. Rollins has made many attempts to find photographs of the Bingham paintings burned in this fire, but apparently none are extant. The student of Bingham must be content with contemporary accounts.

During the spring of 1861 Bingham became more and more perturbed over the political and social conditions then dividing his country. He writes from St. Louis on March 6, 1861:

". . . Old Abe appears reasonable in his inaugural and I hope he will be sustained in the discharge of his duty. He perhaps should not have said more, and I don't think he ought to have said less. I am tired of submission to traitors. If they will force a war I am for giving them enough of it. . . ."

By June 5 his work had so diminished in quantity that he informs his friend, from Kansas City:

". . . We are all out of employment, and Art is far below everything else in such times as these. I am ready to turn my attention for the time being, to any thing by which I can keep from sinking in debt and secure the bare necessaries of life for those who have a right to look to me for support.

"I have just written to Blair at St. Louis and to Mr. Bates in Washington soliciting their influence in procuring me a clerkship or position as draughtsman in some department of engineering associated with the army or elsewhere. . . ."

He received for the summer a captaincy in the Irish Company of Van Horn's Battalion of United States Volunteer Corps. This organization was formed to preserve order in Kansas City. He evidently was not happy in this work.

"Kansas City June 29, 1861

". . . At the unanimous call of the members of the company I have consented to serve them as Captain, and have commenced the duties of the office. You know that such a position is not in harmony with my tastes, nor does my education qualify me for the duties pertaining to it; but this *great emergency* of our country requires us to imitate the example of our Fathers, and I yield myself, with the best ability which I possess, to any service which may be required from me. . . ."

He resigned his captaincy in Kansas City and was appointed State Treasurer by Governor Gambel, January 4, 1862. On January 22, from the Treasurer's Office in Jefferson City, Bingham writes this interesting, well-phrased sentiment: "I am *conditionally* for men though unconditionally for the *Union*."

On August 13, 1862, Bingham gives to his sister, Mrs. Amanda Barnes of Arrow Rock, his position concerning the war.

"In answer to your request in behalf of the boys I send the within papers which were written exclusively by myself at the beginning of the Rebellion. This *war*, they may rest assured, is simply an effort of one party to destroy the government established by our Fathers and attested by experience, *on the one side*, and an effort to maintain it by those who regard it as the last hope of freedom on the other side. The authors of the Rebellion knew very well that Southern people were easily excited upon the subject of Slavery, and that lawless efforts on the part of Northern abolitionists to destroy the efficacy of laws of Congress in their favor furnished grounds for uneasiness. They therefore told us that the national government was the enemy of Slavery and proposed its destruction in defiance of the constitution. These same authors of the Rebellion, however, send their ambassadors to Europe, where they well knew that the public sentiment was opposed to Slavery, and these ambassadors are instructed to tell the people *there* that the Government of the United States is a *proslavery* government, and that even the black Republican Congress with but one dissenting vote had pledged the perpetuation of Slavery in states where it existed. What they have told us, or what they have told the people of Europe, one or the other must be false, and should we be such fools as to be seduced into a rebellion against the government established by Washington and other great men of the South by the statements of men who are so plainly seen to be liars? At the very commencement of the war, I was the first Missourian in the border counties to enter the service of the government as a private. I have seen much on the part of men proposing to be Unionists which I have been compelled to condemn; but the same may be said of the professed votaries of Christianity, and does this justify us in becoming infidels? If my nephews follow my advice, those of them old enough to shoulder a musket and pull a trigger will volunteer in the service of the U. S. This is the best thing they can now do for themselves and country. If they associate with Secessionists and believe their statements, they will likely side with treason. I would suffer death sooner than counsel them to dishonor. If they will go into the army either for nine months or during the war and will come to me, I will assist them." [19]

In celebration of the capture of Camp Jackson, May 10, 1861, the artist painted *General Nathaniel Lyon and General Frank P. Blair Starting from the Arsenal Gate in St. Louis to Capture Camp Jackson* (Plate XI, No. 2). This painting is now the property of the G. B. Rollins estate.

Still serving his term as State Treasurer, Bingham corresponds with his friend from Jefferson City. He is evidently fatigued and discouraged with the job.[20]

"Jefferson City Dec. 21, 1863

". . . The business of my office has vastly increased and keeps me so constantly engaged that I scarcely have time to do or think about anything else. Unless the salary shall be doubled I do not think anyone qualified for the office will hereafter seek it. If you can find me a vacant foreign mission, or obtain me a commission to paint a better picture, than that by Leuitze, for the Capitol at Washington, I will resign. . . ."

Judge North Todd Gentry, Columbia, Missouri, lawyer and historian, when questioned about Bingham's tenure of office as State Treasurer, said, "I have looked into the records of that office at the time that Bingham was treasurer. Certainly he was an honest man—in a position where a weaker man would have been tempted—but he was not at all trained, nor temperamentally suited, to do that work."

Order No. 11

"During Bingham's incumbency as treasurer, General Thomas Ewing, who was in command of the Department of the Border, with headquarters at Kansas City, issued his famous 'General Order No. 11' (Plate XIII) August 25, 1863. Bingham was outraged at the unwarranted severity of this order and went at once to Kansas City and had an interview with Ewing, urging him to rescind it. Ewing refused to do this, and the interview became acrimonious. Bingham left, saying; 'If you persist in executing that order, I will make you infamous with pen and brush as far as I am able.'"[21]

Residing at Independence after the completion of his term as treasurer, Bingham was at work in November, 1865, upon that polemic canvas which had subsequent widespread influence, *Order No. 11*.[22]

Bingham was a great-hearted man, willing, even eager, to fight for what he deemed to be the right, but he was charitable to his enemies and ever quick to forget his attitude toward the South after the war.

"Independence July 10, 1867

". . . We are making very extensive preparations for a great barbecue which is to come off near this city on the 24th of this month. Our object is to bring about a fraternal feeling in place of the animosity engendered by the war, but the chief end is to aid the widows & orphans of deceased confederate soldiers, for whom a *Home* has been instituted in our county. . . ."

But his vehement objection to the cruel Order No. 11, issued by General Ewing was given expression in the painting of that name. This he began upon a cloth-covered wooden panel. Soon afterward he began another picture, this time using a linen tablecloth as the canvas. This picture, which he completed first, is the original from which the engraving was made.

According to Mr. C. B. Rollins, his father and Colonel R. B. Price loaned $5,000 to Bingham to have the painting engraved by Sartain. Because financial depression caused the people to regard an engraved print as a luxury not essential to comfortable living, the engravings did not sell well and Bingham could not meet his obligation. Major Rollins, deeming it a privilege to help his friend again, paid Price for his share of the picture and thus became the sole owner. Later he presented the picture to his son, George Bingham Rollins, in whose home it remained for over thirty years. This painting is now owned by the heirs of George Bingham Rollins and is stored in the William Rockhill Nelson Gallery, Kansas City.

The cloth-covered panel painting was probably completed at a later date and became the possession of Mrs. J. W. Mercer, Independence, Missouri, from whom it was purchased by Mr. Paul Gardner, representing the William Rockhill Nelson Gallery of Art.

In *Order No. 11* Bingham is guilty of false rhetoric and indulges in exaggerated pathos. The scene shows the Union officers ejecting the family of a defiant Southern gentleman from their stately home. In the foreground the head of the family, surrounded by his abjectly pleading daughters and mourning retainers, is gesturing, unsubmissive, to the bullying Union officer. Back of this overdramatic group is pictured the staff of soldiery looting the home, preparatory to the burning. All this mass is balanced on the right by a procession of refugees who, having loaded their earthly goods upon carts and wagons, are looking pathetically forward to any miserable shelter. The background is heavy with smoke from the many burning homes of the unfortunate people.

No sketches can be found that coincide with any of the figures within this composition. Unquestionably, Bingham did not bother to do this preliminary work, and the drawing suffers as a consequence. Artistically, this picture lacks that quality which shows Bingham at his best.

During the next years Bingham frequently, by word of mouth and by writing, defended his interpretation of the sinfulness of this order. On December 23, 1867, Bingham replied to one Reverend R. S. Johnson:

". . . These facts of history, such as I have presented on my canvas, have no necessary connexion with the sale of negroes by Yankees, or their purchase by Southerners. They teach a lesson which previous history had taught our fathers, but which our children of future generations should understand, namely: that the tendencies of Military power are anti-republican and despotic, and that to preserve Liberty and secure its blessings, the supremacy of Civil Authority must be carefully maintained." [23]

Again, on March 17, 1869, Bingham is forced to argue his cause.
"To the Editor of the Republican:

"I have reason to complain of a criticism contained in the Democrat of the 11inst., on my picture entitled 'Civil War.' It is grossly unjust. The writer either wilfully misrepresents or wholly missapprehends my design in placing upon canvass one of the most memorable incidents of the war. Whatever may have been the motive which prompted the promulgation of 'Order No. 11,' it is very certain that it had no basis in law, justice, or humanity. The effect of it was not only the depopulation, but the desolation of one of the fairest and most highly cultivated districts in our State. The people, indiscriminately, were compelled to abandon their homes—men, women, and children. Their dwellings were plundered and then burned to the ground. Their farming utensils, their household goods, their stock, and every species of portable property, were seized and taken into Kansas and appropriated to the private uses of the plunderers.

"It made no difference whether a man was for or against his Government; all had to go who lived within the limits embraced by the order. Well-known Union men were not only robbed, but murdered in cold blood, and the design of my picture is not 'to perpetuate a diseased idea of an historical event' (as alleged by the Democrat), but to present its severe and rugged features in the enduring forms of art, and thus hand over to eternal infamy the perpetrators and defenders of outrages which scarcely find a parallel in the annals of the most barbarous ages. I deny that I have pictured those entitled to be called 'Union military men' as 'brutal, repulsive, soulless beings.' I lived in that district of the country, knew its people and all the prominent facts of its history during the war. I was myself a Union soldier, as was every male member of my family capable of bearing arms, and would, therefore, be the last man to libel a class, either with pen or pencil, who were my comrades in arms— the honest, the brave, the patriotic defenders of the constitutional government of our fathers in its time of need and peril. Such men are entitled to and have my highest respect.

"The writer of the criticism endeavors to make it appear that the central figure in my foreground group is intended to represent the 'rebels of that region,' but there is nothing in the figure or its surroundings that warrants his assumption. To those whose visions are unclouded by prejudice, it represents that large class of law-abiding men who are known as honest and thrifty cultivators of the soil, standing where they have a right to stand, at their own homes, and where the Government was bound, in honor and justice, to protect them in all their rights of person and property. Instead of this, their thrift was reckoned as rebellion, and without being charged with, or convicted of crime, were robbed or murdered as the whim of their persecutors might dictate.

"The scene in the picture is but one of hundreds of a similar character, and the charred remains of broken walls and solitary chimneys yet to be seen all over that fearfully desolated region, attest the truth of my delineations, and would cause any other than the art critic of the Democrat to blush at attempting to discredit them.

"To classify the brutal actors in such scenes as 'Union military men' is an insult to every honest soldier who periled his life in defence of his flag. They were the 'Red Legs' of Kansas, and their equally demoniac associates, known only as thieves and assassins, in whose judgment all men owning property

[105]

were sufficiently rebels to be robbed and murdered.

"The critic tells us that 'good men should strive to heal all the bitterness of the past and learn to forget its harsh features.' Yet in the same breath in which he thus moralizes and inculcates charity and obliviousness, he speaks of 'demoniac harpies of that region who rushed forth in darkness and by surprise to wreak their bloody vengeance upon all who dared to be true to the Government'—of men 'the recital of whose cowardly and atrocious crimes no civilized land can equal.'

"In what can such statements differ from mine in the effect of arousing 'old passions,' unless the public yields a credence to mine which it has learned to withhold from those of the critic? He labels his scoundrels 'rebels and bushwhackers,' while I more appropriately, because in accordance with the peculiar province of art, designate mine by the brand which nature has stamped them, and the distinguished garb in which they choose to be arrayed.

"He is right in saying that 'the mission of true art is to exalt emotions, kindle pure purposes, and inspire to nobleness,' but it will never be able to do this by making crime respectable, or by giving to scoundrels the rank due only to honest men. The great Leonardi Divinci, in his immortal painting of the 'Last Supper' placed the repulsive face of Judas in close proximity to the benign countenance of the Prince of Peace.

"It is thus that I present virtue and vice in my picture, the brightness and divinity of the former appearing only the more conspicuous as relieved by the dark and satanic features of the latter.

"I am sorry to perceive that the critic still retains a fraternal regard for the wretches whom he upheld, and whose atrocities he encouraged during the war. He need not fear, however, that his favorites will suffer from any 'old passions' which my picture may arouse against them. A large number of them have been hung, and thus placed beyond the reach of any effect which can spring from human passion. Some of them linger in the darkness and solitude of prisons, and the remainder are skulking in remote districts, where, their crimes, being unknown, are not likely to bring upon them the retribution which they merit.

"G. C. BINGHAM" [24]

Just as opinion was divided concerning this attack upon a United States Army policy, so there were some who defended it vigorously and proclaimed its popularity, such as the *Missouri Statesman* of January 1, 1869. Frank James, brother of the notorious Jesse James, supposedly said: "And Order No. 11—Ewing's, I am glad General Bingham put on immortal

DR. BENOIST TROOST

PLATE XII
NO. 1

VINNIE REAM

PLATE XII
NO. 2

canvas. That is a picture that talks. That order simply ruined hundreds of peaceful homes in western Missouri. I know one man up in Jackson County who made a fortune going around picking up cattle that had been abandoned, a high-toned cattle thief." [25]

July, 1866, Bingham, again motivated by his conviction that the Republican government was not wisely setting about on a program of reconstruction but prompted sometimes by unworthy, hateful prejudice, was engaged in painting the picture of *Major Dean in Jail*. The Reverend Dean, a pastor and a loyal Unionist, was incarcerated for preaching without having sworn the oath of loyalty to the Union. [26]

The canvas reveals the dignified minister sitting upon a stool before the barred window of his cell. He is reading the Bible and near him lies a crumpled paper, probably the *Baptist Journal*. The bare cell contains nothing else but a meager mattress and blanket. The picture, now owned by Mr. W. E. Thomas, Kansas City, was painted upon a fairly durable sheet of hot-press paper and is still well preserved.

The artist at this period of his life was deeply troubled by the idea that Christian principles, in which he was a firm believer, were not always observed by the victors in the years following the war. He felt that a sincere forgiveness and a wise forgetting would have profited the Union causes so much more.

Bingham's active mind kept him continually aware of the issues at stake in those turbulent times when one's political beliefs seemed so much more fundamental than they do today. Not only did the artist contemplate the scene and intelligently gauge the principles involved, but he was also participating actively in matters of state. He submitted his name to the state Congressional nominating committee as candidate from his district, but he was not appointed. Two years later he represented his district, however, as Democratic elector. He had been, of course, a loyal Whig before this time, but the unfortunate incidents after the war caused him to transfer his allegiance to the opposing party.

Besides these political activities during and following the war, Bingham was occupied steadily, of course, with that profession which gained him his livelihood, portrait painting. He painted many portraits of a more personal and intimate nature, such as the likenesses of his son, Rollins Bingham, and the baby, John Mastin. Many of the important people of the state sat for him, so that during this period he received as clients Mr. Thomas H. Mastin and Mr. Frank P. Blair. In speaking of the portrait of Blair, Bingham writes:

"I think it is by far the most striking full-length portrait that I have painted. I have endeavored to give the head all the rugged force which nature has bestowed upon the original, and I have given the figure the bearing and attitude which would mark it as Blair's even if the head were out of sight. You will hardly dislike even the pantaloons which, by letting out a few stitches in some places and taking in a few in others, I place my tailorship on a par with my art."

When the portrait, even though not quite completed, was exhibited it was received with high praise. The comment upon it, to be found in the *Jefferson City People's Tribune* of January 25, 1871, speaks not only of the excellent quality of the painting, but also gives to us an idea of the popularity of Bingham throughout the country at the time.

"Mr. Bingham

"This distinguished artist is now spending a few days in town. His studio is at Miss Lusk's, where may be seen the portraits of Gen. Blair and some of our own citizens. The portrait of Blair is to be full length when completed and even in its present incomplete condition is pronounced by many to be superior to the portrait painted some years ago by Boyle. We are authorized by Mr. Bingham's friends to say that he will paint the portraits of all who may desire it.

"The famous picture of the Civil War (*Order No. 11*), which has already won a national reputation, is now on exhibition at Dr. Riddler's Drug Store, and is valued by artists at $7,000. In compliance with a general demand, it is now being engraved on steel. Copies, from $10 upwards. Subscriptions for these will be received at Dr. Riddler's."

In 1870, then in his fifty-ninth year, Bingham moved from Independence to Kansas City, where he resided for the remaining years of his life.

Probably in answer to a request by Major Rollins that Bingham give the latter some information concerning art, which the lawyer evidently wished to use in a speech he was planning to present, the artist writes his friend the following letter:

"Kansas City June 19 1871

"Maj J. S. Rollins
"My dear Sir
  "Since I received your last I have been considerably indisposed and have also had my mind engaged by some out of door matters requiring attention. I have never been able to write any thing about Art in a manner satisfactory to myself, and I believe the same is the case, to a great extent, with nearly all Artists.
  "Ruskin became the popular writer on Art only after he had totally failed as a painter, and notwithstanding his captivating style some of the best artists regard his writings as barren of truth as his pictures. I feel my inability to aid you but am comforted with the thought that you do not need my assistance. Your natural love of Art and what you have seen of it will not allow you to be at fault in giving it the finest drapery which words can afford. You can justly assume that it is the highest expression of the human mind as it is filled and moved by the love of all that is beautiful in the widest sense of the latter term, and that as it invariably forms the crowning chaplet of the most advanced civilization we can reasonably expect that it will fulfill its proper mission upon our continent in the production of monuments which will rival in excellence all that human genius has been able to accomplish else-where. Our brief past sufficiently indicates this. In historical painting, the works of West, Trumbul, Copley and Alston rank with the most successful efforts of European Artists. In portraiture, Stewart and lately Elliott and many others have left us delineations of the 'human face divine' which come fully up to all that can be required in that department. The productions of our landscape painting will not suffer in comparison with any that the pencil of Claude or Turner has left to the world. You can indeed almost safely as-sert that in our Church we have the greatest of landscape painters whether of the old or modern masters. His 'Heart of the Andes' & 'Falls of Niagara' seem literal presentations of Nature as she appears in all her transcendant beauty & sublimity. They are scarcely pictures, but rather Nature herself as seen through the eyes of her most devoted worshiper. We have also our Hogarths and our Wilkies. The graphic outlines of Darley. The humorous productions of Mount and others as seen in the 'Bargaining for a horse' 'The Jolly Flat-Boatmen' and County Election,' assure us that our social and po-

[109]

litical characteristics as daily and annually exhibited will not be lost in the lapse of time for want of an Art record rendering them full justice. Your sojourn at Washington and visits to our Art galleries in other cities makes you as familiar with our sculptors and their works as I am. Crawford whose genius has left us the Washington monument at Richmond, perhaps towers above them all. Unfortunately death took him from us when his greatest purposes were yet unaccomplished.

"You are well acquainted with Mills and can do justice to his merits. You are also acquainted with the wonderful little girl (Vinnie Ream) whose works I have not seen but whose rare merits will assure her a proper niche in your address.

"Upon the whole I am confident that whatever you may say about our Art and Artists will be well said and worthy of the subject. I do not couple my own name with my works mentioned in the foregoing, as I can fully trust it to you to do with it just as you please. . . ."

A photostatic copy of the first page is shown on the page facing. Bingham's penmanship, precise and clear, did not alter to any degree throughout his lifetime. His letter forms are drawn with the identical simplicity and are written in the same style throughout the decades that he corresponded with his friend. Each letter has a note of pleasant formality about it. Not once in their correspondence of nearly half a century did the artist fail to address Rollins as "Major J. S. Rollins, My dear Sir."

In the fall of 1871 a group of admiring friends of Major Rollins requested Bingham to paint the portrait of the man who had given so much to "the State, the texture of whose history was so deeply colored by the thread of his life." [27] Bingham began this portrait of his friend immediately and completed it in the spring of 1873.

"It was a life-sized portrait representing the *Pater Universitatis* standing in the attitude of delivering a speech, a motive suggested by his extended services in the Legislature and Congress. A window at one side disclosed a view of the University, so recalling his acts which brought so much benefit to that institution. The work was enthusiastically lauded at the time as the artist's highest attainment in portraiture. And it is reasonable to believe that his great affection for the man and his familiarity with his features and characteristics should have enabled him to reach the

Kansas City June 19 1871

Maj J. S. Rollins

My dear Sir

Since I received your
last I have been considerably indisposed and
have also had my mind engaged by some out
of door matters requiring attention. I have never
been able to write any thing about Art in a manner
satisfactory to myself, and I believe the same is
the case, to a great extent, with nearly all Artists.

Ruskin became the popular writer on Art only
after he had totally failed as a painter, and not—
withstanding his captivating style some of the
best Artists regard his writings as barren of
truth as his pictures. I feel my inability to aid
you but am comforted with the thought that you
do not need my assistance. Your natural love of
Art and what you have seen of it will not allow
you to be at fault in giving it the finest drapery
which words can afford You can justly
assume that it is the highest expression of the human
mind as it is filled and moved by the love of all
that is beautiful in the widest sense of the latter
term, and that as it invariably forms the crown—
ing Chaplet of the most advanced Civilization

zenith of his power as a portrait painter in this picture. It was destroyed in the University fire of 1892; but a small study in oil remains." [28] This small canvas is now hanging in the library of the C. B. Rollins home, Columbia, Missouri.

The bust portrait (Plate XIV, No. 1) which Bingham completed in 1871 illustrates pictorially what the biographer of the Major wrote as a tribute to the man whom he had known intimately for many years.

"In person the subject of this memorial was tall and commanding. His frame was well proportioned, neither slender nor inclined to fullness. Lithe, but compact and firmly knit in all its members, it lent itself freely to the service of his soul, enduring arduous and unremitting exertion with patience. His facial features were boldly and cleanly cut, the nose, slightly aquiline, bespeaking a Roman energy, set between deep and penetrating eyes of iron-gray, beneath a brow broad and full, and a forehead heaved dome-like upward; the hair dark brown, abundant, and vigorous, while the lower face was muffled in a beard worn full, long, and heavy. He never disdained the elegancies of toilet, while his knightly bearing and gracious address were such as might well have beseemed some courtier in the days of romance. But this gentle gallantry was far from being merely formal or superficial. It was a part of his nature, and struck its roots into his heart; hence it was that the native nobility of his carriage was matched by the genuine benignity of his countenance. Altogether his presence was a striking one, and would have been noted in any assemblage, social or political, as distinguished and conspicuous." [29]

Quite a number of the members of the fine old families of Columbia had their portraits done by the artist during this period. Among them were the wife of Major Rollins and his daughter, Sallie Rodes Rollins.

While Bingham was visiting in the home of Major Rollins, he sketched quite frequently for the entertainment of the children. Mr. C. B. Rollins has in his possession an old and battered scrapbook in which he has preserved many of these delightful remembrances of Bingham's humorous attentions. There are pencil sketches of heads of old men, of Venuses, children, and grazing cows. Artistically they are of no great importance, but they reveal something indescribably intimate about the artist's personality.[30]

In the early winter of 1871 Bingham again visited in Philadelphia, and on December 24 he writes from Sartain's studio:

". . . I arrived safely in this city night before last, and am, at this writing in Sartain's Studio, he working on our plate (of *Order No. 11*) but a few feet from me. He thinks he will have it completed in about two weeks, but if I were not here I think it likely his weeks would go into months, as there are continual calls upon him for other work. . . . The plate is in a very good condition at present, and I think it will require very little correction from me. . . ."

Again, on January 7, 1872, there is a letter concerning his painting *Washington Crossing the Delaware*.

". . . He (Sartain) seems quite anxious to engrave my picture of 'Washington Crossing the Delaware' which is now finished and of which I gave him a photograph. He thinks it would find a large sale here and in New York, and is disposed to engrave it as a partnership matter or a half interest in the copyright. He thinks it far superior to Leuitzes picture of the same subject. . . ."

A letter revealing much of Bingham's insight into personality and showing his ability to analyze good-humoredly the many intricacies of human relations, was written on January 17.

". . . Sartain is still laboring on our plate and thinks he will certainly finish it this week, but this I doubt, as he invariably fails as to time, and now that I am here, I mean to see that the work is made as perfect as possible.

"I labored all last week in retouching and correcting the proof in its then state, so as to make it precisely what I want it to be, and this corrected proof he has now before him, and when the details of his plate are so worked up as to print precisely like the result will be entirely satisfactory. I gave him the portion of your letter in reference to the tardiness of his work and feeling as he must do, that he has not done us entire justice, I am well assured that he will give his entire time to the work until it shall be completed. He seems to be a thorough gentleman, but one of those who have not the fortitude to say no to friends who continually call upon him for services, which when yielded, render it impossible for him to comply with his engagements to those at a distance who cannot stimulate him by their personal presence. . . ."

ORDER NO. 11

Plate XIII

After supervising the completion of the engraving of *Order No. 11* the artist returned to his home in Kansas City and informed Rollins on May 10 that all of the subscribers seem delighted with the engraving and pay promptly as the prints are delivered to them.

Sometime during the summer of 1872 Bingham and his wife must have made a trip to Colorado, for on October 26 a communication from Denver contains the information that the artist has completed a canvas which today is well known as *View of Pike's Peak.*[31] This picture is now in the possession of the Findlay Art Company, Kansas City, Missouri.

Since Bingham was inspired by the grandeur of the Colorado mountain scenery, he probably painted a number of landscapes depicting the beauty which is to be seen in the territory surrounding Denver. According to Rollins Bingham, son of the artist, four of these canvases were owned by Mrs. J. M. Piper in 1902.[32]

Having returned to his home, Bingham writes from Kansas City, November 20, informing Mr. Rollins that he will order a canvas from the East for Rollins' portrait and plans, if he remains at home, to finish it during the winter. He does complete it, for he writes again on March 24, 1873:

". . . During the five or six weeks past I have been constantly at work on your portrait and have just completed it. As soon as it is sufficiently dry I will roll it up and take it to Columbia. When unrolled it may require some little retouching which I can give then.

"I have felt a deep personal interest in the work and have spared no effort to make it such as will give to the future youth of our state a correct idea of the man to whom they will be so much indebted. . . ."

In a state of precarious health, the artist addressed his friend on June 31, 1873:

". . . Doct Wood tells me that I must go to the mountains and I have made up my mind to follow his advice as soon as I can make arrangements to do so, there to remain until my health shall be permanently restored. I perceive from the Statesman of Friday that your portrait has been tendered to the Board of Curators. I am anxious to know what action was taken upon it. In order to remove it to the University I think it will be necessary to roll it up. If this should be required no one should attempt it but myself. . . ."

August 3, 1873, Bingham, after revealing plans for exhibiting two pictures at Louisville, Kentucky, writes his appreciation for the splendid tribute paid to him by A. J. Conant in his speech in behalf of the Board of Curators of the University of Missouri upon the presentation of the portrait of Major Rollins by the people of Columbia.

". . . On yesterday I received a letter from J. D. Osborne Esq. of Louisville, Ky. asking me to send some of my pictures to their exposition which opens on the 5th of September, and thinking it would afford a favorable opportunity to obtain subscribers to our engraving, I concluded that I would send them the large picture (*Order No. 11*) and also my picture of 'Crossing the Delaware' . . .

"I received today the proceedings and speeches upon the occasion of the presentation of your portrait.[33] They send us to immortality together. Conant's allusion to myself was such as became a true artist, devoted to Art and generous to its professors. . . ."

The Puzzled Witness, though still not quite completed, was exhibited in St. Louis on December 11, 1874. "It is another picture of Western life, which might be classed along with the 'Election Series.' At a table, which occupies the center of the picture, sit the two attorneys. To our right stands the puzzled witness, scratching his head in his perplexity, while the dog at his feet shares in his bewilderment. Close about is a crowd of spectators, some only curious, others, either in a critical or a sympathetic manner, intently interested in the trial. Above, at his high bench, sits the all-important fat old judge, with water pitcher and glass at hand, careful, as always, for his physical comfort. The composition is built up in the common pyramidal form; but the apex, which is formed by the judge, is not the point of greatest interest. It is placed somewhat in the shadow, while the greater light falls upon the witness." [34]

The puzzled witness is holding his right hand to a bandaged eye and seems to be in a greatly distressed frame of mind. With hat in hand, he is telling a woeful story, heckled by the smart lawyer who causes him to stumble over his facts.

This painting is now owned by Mr. Huston Crittenden, Kansas City, a relative of the early owner, Judge James M. Gibson.[35] It is difficult to determine why Bingham attempted genre scenes of this type. Although he did prepare a preliminary sketch for the figure of the witness, it is possible that most of the figures in the painting were "types," creations from the artist's mind. It is not one of the best of Bingham's works, certainly, and may have occupied his time while he was reflecting, with amusement, upon some court scene he had witnessed. Many of the faces of the figures are caricatured to the point of coarseness.

At best, *The Puzzled Witness* may be considered one of the minor attempts of the painter, created in an off-moment.

The Last Years

BINGHAM was chosen to serve upon Kansas City's first Board of Police Commissioners in May, 1874. Shortly after his appointment he writes:

"Kansas City May 26, 1874

". . . Our city like all other places is experiencing the effects of hard times, and we have been especial sufferers in that portion of the city in which my interest lies, by the numerous gambling hells and kindred establishments which have been lawlessly tolerated therein by our authorities, and which by driving proper business to other quarters have reduced my rents to a bare sufficiency to pay taxes and insurance, if indeed they shall prove sufficient for that. The result is that I have been compelled to paint portraits this winter for the support of my family, and the prospect is, that I will have to do so for sometime to come. . . ."

On June 7, Bingham reveals his attitude toward the profession of portrait painting; and, of course, it must be assumed that he was writing of the portraits of those people in whom he had no particular interest, in which task he would receive no compensation whatsoever excepting a monetary one. "I am now engaged daily in the studio, painting portraits, as the common phrase among the artists 'to make the pot boil.'"

It is very possible that for many years people will continue to discover Bingham portraits throughout the states. But it seems reasonable that the most important works of this nature have already been collected. That any further inclusion of "pot boilers" would tend to improve Bingham's reputation or teach us to know the artist better is improbable. Time after time Bingham was outspoken concerning his attitude in regard to hack portrait work. It must be remembered that his family was dependent upon him and that this was his way of winning a living.

In 1875 the artist received from Charles H. Hardin, governor of Missouri, the appointment of Adjutant General. It was his sad task to investigate the authenticity of claims of ex-soldiers and their families upon the Government. He performed this task thoroughly, not sparing himself nor the individuals who falsely presented their pleas.

Bingham was sent to Washington in the spring of 1876 to try to push through Congress a bill providing for the reimbursement to the state of money which had been paid to state militia who served under federal direction. He was honored to receive this commission, and was frequently lauded as a citizen, patriotic, unselfish and industrious.

"The Hon. George C. Bingham, who has been spending some time in Washington endeavoring to get the military claims of the people of Missouri allowed, writes that he thinks the National Legislature will yield to the demand.

"A better and more befitting agent to look after these claims could not have been appointed by our worthy Governor. The name of George C. Bingham is one that is known and highly honored beyond the confines of our own State. He is a citizen of patriotic impulses, unselfish in all the purposes of his life, pure in heart, mature in experience, a man of extraordinarily good judgment, and laborious in research. No man in Missouri has toiled with greater energy than he to promote the general welfare of the people of his State.

"A man of his mental and moral organization must necessarily hold to the views embodied in the Democratic notion of the theory of our government; but then he has withal, broad, liberal, comprehensive, generous and patriotic aims that elevate him above mere party considerations, and which exempt him from any measurement by the standard common to mere partizans. George C. Bingham would not, for the highest official position within the gift of the people of the United States, resort to the ordinary and vulgar means practiced in our party politics. It is refreshing to believe that some men of that stamp are yet spared to our country." [1]

During this period in Washington the artist wrote quite frequently to his old friend in Columbia. On April 13, he tells Rollins that he has begun work on the portrait of Vinnie Ream [2] (Plate XII, No. 2).

This portrait is now hanging in the reading room of the Missouri Historical Society, Columbia, Missouri, and shows this charming young girl clothed in a smock, long hair flowing over her shoulders, modeling tool in hand, pausing a moment in her work of making a clay model bust of Lincoln. The portrait is pleasing but has really nothing of exceptional merit to recommend it. It is interesting to note, when studying this portrait, the amount of technical dexterity which Bingham developed during and after his European experience. The hard, sharp planes have disappeared. During these later years the artist worked in sophisticated, but less forceful, manner. It is a neatly done, professional job.

In Kansas City again on October 15, 1876, the grief-stricken artist reveals to his friend that his wife has become mentally deranged, having delusions of a queer nature. It will be necessary, he thinks, to have her committed to the asylum at Fulton. She died there on the third of November.

Rusk tells an interesting story about Bingham's interest in spiritualism shortly after his wife's death. "Bingham himself became somewhat interested a little later in the prevailing excitement over spiritualism. He declared at one time that he had seen and talked to his wife and she had kissed him. 'Ah, she kissed you, did she?' said a friend, 'then she was your wife, indeed; no other woman would kiss such a looking person as you.' Bingham was reared a Methodist, as we have seen, but during his second wife's life, he was united with the Baptist Church. However, he did not readily give up his Methodist habits—he several times communed with other denominations." [3]

From Jefferson City, December 14, 1876, Bingham states his true feelings about holding a public office.

". . . By pursuing my art profession as in the more happy period of my past life I think I will find much greater comfort than attends the discharge of the thankless duties of a public office. I now covet freedom and cheerful society. The latter is especially invaluable to me under my great bereavement, and as an artist I am more likely to have its benefit than when shut up as now in the narrow confines of an office. . . ."

In 1877 Bingham was appointed professor of Art at the University of Missouri.[4] President James Madison Wood of Stephens College, Columbia, Missouri, says that at this time Bingham was also teaching a few art classes at Stephens College. A room was assigned to him in the Normal School Building. Concerning this he writes from Boonville on September 9, 1877, just before the opening of the school year:

". . . In regard to the room designated for my use as a studio but little change will be necessary other than such as will be required for neatness and comfort. As, when established there, I will be frequently visited by strangers and others the studio should be somewhat tastefully fitted up and furnished in harmony with the purpose for which it is intended. A number of plaster casts from antique statuary should be around as models for pupils in art. They are indeed indispensible, as without them the mind of the student cannot be properly imbued with those ideas of grace, elegance and truth which form the basis of genuine art. These casts are not very costly, and may perhaps be obtained in St. Louis. It will be best for me to give my personal attention to their selection.

"I can have my own pictures sent down from Kansas City and placed on the walls. . . ."

From the Lykins Institute, Kansas City, November 4, 1877, Bingham expresses his desire to be a member of the delegation representing the United States at the Paris Exposition.

". . . I perceive that Congress has appropriated $150,000 for the purpose of having the U. S. properly represented at the Paris Exposition. I presume the appointment of the delegates will devolve on the President and if so I would like to be an appointee from our state.

"I believe by writing to your friend Schurtz and others who may have influence with the President, you can likely secure my appointment as a delegate. My being an artist of long standing reputation and now professor of Art in the University of Missouri ought to give strength to my claims. I suppose you can have me recommended by Doct. Laws and professors of our University and also by your friend Doct. Reed. . . ."

Unfortunately, Bingham was not successful in obtaining this appointment.

It was probably during this visit in Kansas City that Bingham became seriously interested in Mrs. Mattie, widow of Dr. Lykins of Kansas City, for on January 3, 1878, Bingham alludes to her as "more than a friend." On June 18 they were married.[5]

On November 3, 1878, Bingham tells Major Rollins in a letter from Lykins Institute that he has been appointed commissioner to select the design for the Robert E. Lee Monument Association of the State of Virginia. Three weeks later he and his wife arrived in Richmond where they remained for about two weeks.

In Columbia, during February, 1879, Bingham was laid low with a severe attack of pneumonia. This illness probably weakened him considerably and was instrumental in causing his premature death early in the summer. While confined to his rooms Bingham wrote an interpretation of his conception of Art. It was written to be given as one of the University Series of Public Lectures, but was delivered by Major Rollins because of Bingham's illness.

Like many artists, Bingham wrote about an aesthetic which was far from the philosophy of art which he incorporated in his own work. Quite evidently, the artist had not thought seriously about putting into abstract conception his ideas of "the ideals of art." He borrowed too much, and not wisely enough.

"Art, the Ideal of Art, and the Utility of Art

"Ladies, Gentlemen and Students of the University:

"I have been requested by our worthy president to embody in a brief lecture, and present to you some of the views on Art which I have been led to entertain from many years of practice and experience and familiarity with the works of many of its most eminent professors. We are all naturally disposed to prefer that mode of expression by which we can communicate to others, most forcibly and clearly, the thought to which we are prompted to give utterance. Hence artists have generally been averse to giving a mere verbal expression to ideas which they are able to present in a far more satisfactory manner, with the pencil or chisel. It is doubtless owing to this reluctance on their part that the literature of their profession is chiefly the product of theorists who can err in safety under the silence of those who alone have the ability to correct them. These theorists are often laboriously ambiguous even in their definition of Art.

"Micheal Angelo, whose sublime and unrivaled productions, both in painting and sculpture, certainly entitle him to be regarded as good authority in all that related to Art, clearly and unhesitatingly designates it as 'The imitation of nature.'

"The Oxford student, however, who ranks as the ablest and most popular writer upon the subject, undertakes to convince his readers that the imitation of nature so far from being Art, is not even the language of Art. He boldly goes still further and asserts that the more perfect the imitation the less it partakes of the character of genuine Art. He takes the position that Art to

MAJOR J. S. ROLLINS

PLATE XIV
NO. 1

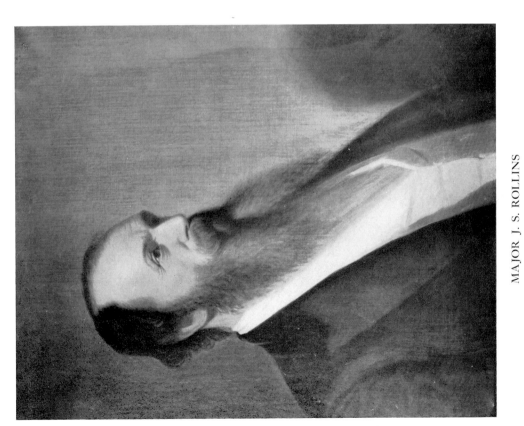

GEORGE CALEB BINGHAM
SELF-PORTRAIT

PLATE XIV
NO. 2

be genuine must be true, and that an imitation of nature so perfect as to produce an illusion, and thereby make us believe that a thing is what it really is not, gives expression to a falsehood, and cannot therefore be justly regarded as genuine Art, an essential quality of which is truth.

"Such logic may be convincing to the minds of those admirers who regard him as an oracle upon any subject which he chooses to touch with his pen. But in all candor it seems to me to be merely on a par with that of a far less distinguished character, who, travelling with a companion along the banks of a river, undertook, for a wager, to convince him that the side of the river on which they were journeying was really the other side. He did it by stating as his postulate that the river had two sides, and as the side opposite to them was one of these sides, the side on which they were travelling was necessarily the other side. Truth and such logic are not always in harmony.

"The well known story of Zenxas and Appeles, two of the most famous painters of ancient Greece, has been handed down to us through the intervening ages. Being rivals and alike ambitious of distinction, a challenge passed between them for a trial of their skill. One painted a picture of grapes so perfect in its imitation of that luscious fruit, that the birds of the air flocked to partake of them as a servant was carrying the picture to the place of exhibition. The other merely painted upon his canvass a curtain, but so perfect was its resemblance to a real curtain, that his rival stretched forth his hand to remove it in order to get a view of the supposed picture beneath. Such an adherence to nature, and I may add to the truth of nature, constitutes what should properly be called the truth of Art; that Art only which belies nature is false Art.

"These imitations are recorded in the literature of that classic period, as evidence of the excellence in Art by which it was characterized. We are loth to suppose in an age made illustrious by the highest civilization which the world had then attained, and surrounded by works of Art which coming ages will never surpass, great statesmen, scholars, artists, and literary men could have been so far mistaken in regard to the true nature of Art, as to recognize as an excellence therein, that which was really a defect.

"About the close of the war of 1812 one of the great naval conflicts between the British and American fleets was dramatized upon the stage in the city of Baltimore. The scenery was arranged with all the skill which the most consummate Art could bestow upon it. Even the movements of the vessels and the motion of the waves were closely imitated. An unsophisticated sailor who had participated in such conflicts, happened to be seated in the pit as one of the audience. Becoming absorbed in what was transpiring before him, to an extent which banished all idea of mere stage effect from his mind, he thought he saw one of our vessels beclouded with smoke, and threatened with destruction by the enemies' fleet. His patriotism rose above all considerations of personal safety. He could not rest without an effort to transmit to the imperilled vessel a knowledge of the danger by which it was threatened. This could only be done by taking to the water, he being an excellent swimmer. He sprang up with great excitement, and approaching the stage and shedding his linen as he went, he plunged head foremost into what he took to be water, but it being only a well devised imitation of that element he went through it to the basement about twenty feet below, leaving our vessel to its fate. What man of ordinary intelligence will venture to affirm that scenic Art thus so nearly resembling the reality of nature is less Art on that account?

"More than once in my own experience portraits painted by myself, and placed in windows facing the sun to expedite their drying, have been mistaken for the originals by persons outside, and spoken to as such. Such occurrences doubtless mark the experience of nearly every portrait painter; but none of them ever dreamed that the temporary deception thus produced lessened the artistic merit of such works. The great ability of Ruskin as a writer is generally and justly conceded. He has performed a great work for artists of his own age in destroying that reverence for the works of the old masters which has attributed to them an excellence entirely beyond the reach of modern genius. But no artist can safely accept his teachings as an infallible guide. Artists who expect to rise to anything like eminence in their profession, must study nature in all her varied phases, and accept her both as his model and teacher. He may consider every theory which may be advanced upon the subject nearest to his heart, but he must trust his own eyes and never surrender the deliberate and matured conclusions of his own judgment to any authority however high.

"What I mean by the imitation of nature is the portraiture of her charms as she appears to the eye of the artist. A pictorial statement which gives us distant trees, the leaves of which are all separately and distinctly marked, is no imitation of nature. She never thus presents herself to our organs of vision. Space and atmosphere, light and shadow, stamp their impress on all that we see in the extended fields which she opens to our view, and an omission to present upon our canvass a graphic resemblance of the appearances thus produced, makes it fall short of that truth which should characterize every work of Art. But while I insist that the imitation of nature is an essential quality of Art, I by no means wish to be understood as meaning that any and every imitation of nature is a work of Art.

"Art is the outward expression of the esthetic sentiment produced in the mind by the contemplation of the grand and beautiful in nature, and it is the imitation in Art of that which creates this sentiment that constitutes its expression. The imitation is the word which utters the sentiment. No Artist need apprehend that any imitation of nature within the possibilities of his power will long be taken for what it is not. There are attributes of nature which the highest Art can never possess. In the younger days of Micheal Angelo, soon after his rapidly developing genius had been noised abroad, he visited the studio of an aged sculptor in Florence while he was engaged in giving the finishing touches to the last and noblest of his works. The old man wishing to have an expression of his judgment upon it, exposed it fully to his view allowing the most favorable light to fall upon it. The young Angelo contemplated it for many minutes with wrapped attention, no word passing from his lips. At length turning upon his heel he said *it lacks one thing*, and immediately disappeared. His words fell as a death blow upon the ears of the old man. He had bestowed upon the work the results of his life-long study in the confident expectation that it would transmit his name to posterity, and associate him in history with the greatest Artists of his day. He became gloomy and despondent, soon sickened and was laid on his deathbed. Learning that Micheal Angelo was again in his vicinity he sent him a message inviting him to visit him. When the young sculptor appeared in his presence he reminded him of the remark which he had made at the close of their previous interview, and earnestly entreated him to name the one thing lacking in what he had fondly regarded as the crowning work of his life. I meant, said the younger artist, that it lacked *the gift of speech* and that only! We can well imagine the new life which, at these words instantly sprang up in the soul of the gifted old man, smoothing his passage to that upper and better life to be associated forever with all who love the true and the beautiful.

"As the powers of man are limited so is Art necessarily limited in its domain. It can only embody those appearances of nature which are addressed to the eye and exhibited in form and color. Like the work of the grand old Florentine sculptor it can faithfully present the human form in all its symmetry and beauty, but it can not breathe into that form a living soul or endow it with speech and motion. It can give us the hue and forms of hills, mountains, lakes and rivers, or old ocean, whether in calm, sunshine or storm, but all that we see in these results of limited power is alike motionless and voiceless. There is no murmuring in their brooks as they seem to encounter the rocks in their passage. Their clouds are stationary in their skies, their suns and moons never rise or set. There is no sound of lowing coming from their flocks and herds.

All is silent and still, and being so can never be mistaken for actual nature. Nevertheless that Art which, within the limited sphere of Art, most nearly resembles actual nature, most clearly expresses the sentiment which actual nature produces in the minds of those who have the taste to relish her beauties. Ruskin, with all his verbal powers of description, failed as an artist, and I have no hesitation in affirming that any man who does not regard the imitation of nature as the great essential quality of Art will never make an artist.

"THE IDEAL IN ART"

"There are various and conflicting opinions as to what constitutes the ideal in Art. In the minds of those liberally endowed artists whose productions exhibit a wide range of thought, it seems to my judgment to be that general and much embracing idea necessarily derived from the love and study of nature in her varied and multitudinous aspects, as presented in form and color. It must, however, be necessarily limited by the taste of the artist, which may confine him to what is special rather than to what is general in nature. I say it may be limited and contracted by the taste of the artist. Artists permit themselves to be absorbed only by what they love. And as nature presents herself to them in a thousand phases, they may worship her in few or many. Such of her phases as take possession of their affections also take possession of their minds, and form thereon their ideal, it matters not whether it be animate or inanimate nature, or a portion of either. A Landseer is captivated by the faithfulness, habits and hairy texture of dogs, and makes them his specialty in Art, being kennelled in his mind, as it were, they exclude other subjects of Art and become the ideal which governs his pencil. When Sidney Smith was requested by a friend to sit to Landseer for his portrait he replied, *'is thy servant a dog that he should do this thing?'* His reply was significant of the apprehension justly entertained that the artist could not avoid giving to his portrait something of the expression which more properly belonged to his favorites of the canine species. Rosa Bonhier, early in life, fell in love with the kine which furnishes us all, with the milk, butter and cheese which form so large a portion of the aliment which sustains our physical frames. In living with them and caressing them, their forms and habits took possession of her mind as they had done of her heart, and formed that ideal, which makes her pictures of cattle far transcend in excellence those of Paul Potter or any of her predecessors.

"I cannot believe that the ideal in Art, as is supposed by many, is a specific mental form existing in the mind of the artist more perfect than any prototype in nature, and that to be a great artist he must look within him for a model and close his eyes upon external nature. Such a mental form would be a fixed and determined idea, admitting of no variations, such as we find in diversified nature and in the works of artists most distinguished in their profession. An artist guided by such a form would necessarily repeat in every work exactly the same lines and the same expression.

"To the beautiful belongs an endless variety. It is seen not only in symmetry and elegance of form, in youth and health, but is often quite as fully apparent in decrepit old age. It is found in the cottage of the peasant as well as in the palace of kings. It is seen in all the relations, domestic and municipal, of a virtuous people, and in all that harmonizes man with his Creator. The ideal of the great artist, therefore, embraces all of the beautiful which presents itself in form and color, whether characterized by elegance and symmetry or by any quality within the wide and diversified domain of the beautiful. Mere symmetry of form finds no place in the works of Rembrant, Teniers, Ostade, and others of a kindred school. Their men and women fall immeasurably below that order of beauty which characterizes the sculptures of classic Greece. But they address themselves none the less to our love of the beautiful, and none the less tend to nourish the development and growth of those tastes which prepare us for the enjoyment of that higher life which is to begin when our mortal existence shall end.

"All the thought which in the course of my studies, I have been able to give to the subject, has led me to conclude that the ideal in Art is but the impressions made upon the mind of the artist by the beautiful or Art subjects in external nature, and that our Art power is the ability to receive and retain these impressions so clearly and distinctly as to be able to duplicate them upon our canvas. So far from these impressions thus engraved upon our memory being superior to nature, they are but the creatures of nature, and depend upon her for existence as fully as the image in a mirror depends upon that which is before it. It is true that a work of Art eminating from these impressions may be, and generally is, tinged by some peculiarity belonging to the mind of the artist, just as some mirrors by a slight convex in the surface give reflections which do not exactly accord with the objects before them. Yet any obvious and radical departure from its prototypes in nature will justly condemn it as a work of Art.

"I have frequently been told, in conversation with persons who have obtained their ideas of Art from books, that an artist should give to his productions something more than nature presents to the eye. That in painting a portrait for instance, he should not be satisfied with giving a true delineation of the form and features of his subject, with all the lines of his face which mark his individuality, but in addition to these should impart to his work

[125]

the *soul* of his sitter. I cannot but think that this is exacting from an artist that which rather transcends the limits of his powers, great as they may be. As for myself, I must confess, that if my life and even my eternal salvation depended upon such an achievement, I would look forward to nothing better than death and everlasting misery, in that place prepared for the unsaved. According to all of our existing ideas of a soul, there is nothing material in its composition. The manufacture, therefore, of such a thing out of the earthen pigments which lie upon my palate would be a miracle entitling me to rank as the equal of the Almighty himself. Even if I could perform such a miracle, I would be robbing my sitter of the most valuable part of his nature and giving it to the work of my own hands. There are lines which are to be seen on every man's face which indicate to a certain extent the nature of the spirit within him. But these lines are not the spirit which they indicate any more than the sign above the entrance to a store is the merchandize within. These lines upon the face embody what artists term its expression, because they reveal the thoughts, emotions, and to some extent the mental and moral character of the man. The clear perception and practiced eye of the artist will not fail to detect these; and by tracing similar lines upon the portrait, he gives to it the expression which belongs to the face of his sitter, in doing this, so far from transferring to his canvass the soul of his subject, he merely gives such indications of a soul as appear in certain lines of the human face; if he gives them correctly, he has done all that Art can do.

"THE UTILITY OF ART

"If man were a mere animal whose enjoyments did not extend beyond the gratification of the appetites of such a being Art might justly be regarded as a thing of very little importance.

"In the elevated sense in which we are discussing it, it addresses itself solely to that portion of man which is the breath of the Eternal—which lives forever, —which is capable of endless growth and progress, and the requirements of which are peculiar to itself. The beautiful, and all that is embraced in what is termed esthetics, together with all that contributes to mental development is the natural food of the soul, and is as essential to its growth, expansion and happiness, as is the daily bread we consume, to the health and life of our animal nature. The appetite for this spiritual food, like that for the nourishment essential to our material growth, is a part of our nature. As the latter turns the lips of the new born infant to the breast of its mother, the former exhibits itself in its love of the beautiful. Before it is capable of thought or reason, its eyes will sparkle with intense delight at the presentation of a beautiful bouquet, while it would look upon a nugget of gold richer than the mines of California ever produced, with utter indifference. As the growth, strength and development of the body depend upon the food demanded by its natural appetites, so must the growth and development of the soul, and its capacity for enjoyment, depend upon the spiritual food demanded by those tastes peculiar to and a part of its nature.

"The soul is as necessarily dwarfed by withholding from it its proper nourishment, as is the body from a like cause. The natural wants of both should be constantly supplied, that the child as it grows in stature may also wax strong in spirit. If we regard that as useless which meets the demands of the esthetic tastes of our nature, then we must regard God as exhibiting no wisdom in decorating nature in so lavish a manner with the grand, the sublime, and beautiful. In giving us the fruit he might have omitted the beautiful bloom which heralds its coming. In giving us the rain which moistens our fields and makes our rivers, he might have withheld the accompanying arch which spans the heavens and exhibits to our delighted gaze its perfect symmetry in form and unequaled glory in color. He might have spread over land and sea and sky a dull and monotonous hue, instead of enriching them with that infinitude of the beautiful, which they ceaselessly unveil to the eye of man. All this display of the grand and the beautiful seems to be a divine recognition of the wants of our spiritual nature and a benevolent purpose to supply them.

"The absence of Art in any nation will ever be a mark of its ignorance and degradation. While the highest Art will be the chaplet which crowns the highest civilization, its uses extend far beyond the gratification of our inherent love of the beautiful. As a language, its expressions are clearer than any which can be embodied in alphabetical forms, or that proceeds from articulate sounds. It also has the advantage of being everywhere understood by all nations, whether savage or civilized.

"Much that is of great importance in the history of the world would be lost if it were not for Art. Great empires which have arisen, flourished and disappeared, are now chiefly known by their imperishable records of Art. It is indeed the chief agent in securing national immortality. In the remote and prehistoric periods of the past, there have doubtless been nations who gave no encouragement to Art, but like the baseless fabrics of vision they have disappeared and left not a wreck behind. And this glorious Republic of ours, stretching its liberal sway over a vast continent, will perhaps be best known in the distant ages of the future by the imperishable monuments of Art which we may have the taste and the genius to erect."

Bingham writes from Kansas City, Missouri, May 5, 1879:

". . . I think I have entirely recovered from my severe illness in Columbia, and have been for the past three weeks in painting a full length portrait of a child of Judge Waldo of New Mexico, about the age of your little Ulilee. I have nearly completed it, and if nothing happens, adverse thereto, I will likely be ready to return to Columbia in a week or ten days, to complete my unfinished work there. . . ."

The early part of the summer was spent in his home in Kansas City. Bingham died on July 7, after an attack of cholera morbus.

The Man

GEORGE CALEB BINGHAM was a man blessed with an inquiring mind, an active body, and a will of power. He was a visionary but not an idle dreamer, an analyst but not a malcontent, an actor who was possessed by purpose. He was dominated by the creative spirit.

"In personal appearance, Bingham was not a striking figure. Small of stature, five feet eight inches in height, and weighing never more than one hundred and fifty pounds, of delicate constitution always, there was yet a dynamic quality in the man that distinguished him in any crowd. I think this quality sprang from the fact that he was the very embodiment of moral and physical courage, 'le chevalier sans peur et sans reproche.' " [1]

The self-portrait (Plate XIV, No. 2) painted a few years before his death [2] shows the artist in full front view, drawing board in hand, making some sketch notations with the pencil. The large and well-formed head rises grandly above shoulders slightly bent. He is dressed in the unostentatious manner of the post-Civil War period. A low-collared shirt with black bow tie half hidden under the linen, is the single relief for the somber black of his coat.

The face has the look of a man who is absorbed with all of life. Deeply grooved lines about his mouth and eyes disclose a hint of those years of struggle through which he forced himself, and suggest, too, the tribulation which he was fated to bear, especially during the last two decades of his life. [3] The full and generous mouth indicates the humor which, quick and often tinged with the spice of wit, was characteristic of Bingham. "Though many of us think tomorrow of the fitting remark we might have made today," recounts Mr. C. B. Rollins, "Bingham never hesitated, but quickly and pointedly said what he thought." There are many diverting anecdotes which, told by Mr. Rollins, substantiate this statement about the artist.

[129]

About 1860, Bingham was a frequent visitor at the home of his Columbia intimate. "The time I first recall him, he arrived one evening for a visit, and I, a youngster, was deputed to show him to his room. Filled with my own importance, I walked briskly ahead carrying a candle to light the way, while Bingham followed with his valise and portfolio. I set the candle down, and then with childish curiosity lingered to see what the portfolio, which he had begun to unstrap, might contain. He laid out a few things, and I recall my disappointment at the meager contents. But my curiosity was yet to be satisfied in full measure. After unpacking his artist's materials, he took off his coat and hung it on a chair, went to the bureau, untied and removed his choker, and then to my unspeakable amazement, lifted off the entire top of his head, exposing a great white dome. I was speechless with fright and fled in terror; I had never seen or heard of a wig before. My mother finally quieted my fears by explaining to me that when Mr. Bingham was about nineteen years old, he had a severe attack of measles which left him bald, and ever since, he had worn a wig, the removal of which had given me such a scare. From that hour, Mr. Bingham assumed great importance in my eyes; for *me*, he was a marked man.

"Many years later, after Bingham had been married the third time and had brought his bride to live at Stephens College, Columbia, his wig again played a stellar role. One day at dinner, the waitress in some way caught the button on her sleeve in a curl of Bingham's wig and whisked it half way around the table before it could be recovered—much to the mortification of the bride and to the amusement of the teachers and pupils present. But Bingham, with that philosophy which characterized him through life, remarked that as he could not keep his hair on his head, it was not surprising that others could not keep it on his head.

"We children looked forward with the greatest pleasure to Bingham's visits. He was a lover of children and would tell us stories and illustrate them with sketches of the characters as he went along. Some of these sketches I still have and value highly. Those days, remember, were the dignified, leisurely days of the ante-bellum period—before the hectic rush and turmoil of more recent times. Then, a visit of less than a week from a friend was considered cold treatment, and Bingham frequently came and stayed with us a month or six weeks at a time." [4]

From Mr. C. B. Rollins come to us all of these entertaining personal anecdotes which make a living portrait of the painter.

"Bingham was a man of strong convictions; in fact, his opinions were convictions. And in his mental processes, he was one of the most direct men I ever knew. His mind acted at once on the matter in hand, and he did not wait until tomorrow to decide what he should have said or done in a given case. In this connection, I recall an amusing incident which occurred in 1866. Dr. Read had just become president of the university. At the time, Mr. Bingham, who did not know Dr. Read, was visiting at our house, and my father invited Dr. Read to take dinner and meet Mr. Bingham. There were several gentlemen present, and after a good dinner, everybody was in a talkative humor and the conversation grew very general and intimate. The subject of matrimony came up. Dr. Read, through one of those inexplicable blunders that wise men will sometimes fall into, remarked that he was a monogamist, and that he could think of no more fitting epitaph for himself, nor one he would desire more, than that he was the faithful husband of one wife. Mr. Bingham, who had already been twice married and probably had in the back of his mind that he might marry again should opportunity occur (and it did occur), was on his feet at once. He walked over to Dr. Read, shook his finger in his face and said 'I want you to know, sir, that men whose shoe laces you are not worthy to unloose have been married oftener than once.' It required all the tact and social presence-of-mind of which my father was master to restore harmony. Bingham and Dr. Read later became warm friends and Bingham painted portraits of him and his wife." [5]

Another story which tells of the artist's quick response when he was driven to vexation is told: " . . . When Bingham was adjutant general of Missouri and my father a member of the General Assembly, General William T. Sherman (a brother-in-law, by the way, of General Ewing) visited Jefferson City. While my father was showing Sherman the capitol, they stopped in at Bingham's office and the three went together to the Senate chamber where among other pictures was an equestrian portrait of 'Old Hickory' by Bingham. Sherman, not aware of the authorship of the picture, blurted out in his blunt soldierly fashion: 'The artist has put that horse in an impossible attitude. No horse could ever have gotten into that position.' Bingham looked at him a moment and then replied: 'Have you noticed the rider of that horse? That is "Old Hickory," a great soldier and statesman, sir. He probably had as much to do with the position of that horse as the artist had. If the artist had been painting *you* on horseback, he would probably have placed you astride a gentle, duck-legged pony ambling quietly along a country lane.' " [6]

When Bingham had been appointed professor of art at the University of Missouri he was busy, for a time, painting the portrait of Dr. Laws, who was then president of the University. "In 1876, Dr. Laws had brought here from New York City, to fill the chair of Hebrew and Semitic Literature, Dr. Alexander Meyrowitz a fine, scholarly old gentleman who, though versed in his profession, was woefully lacking in tact. One day he wandered into Bingham's studio, and seeing the portrait of his friend, Dr. Laws, on the easel, began to criticize it with all the assurance of ignorance. Meyrowitz, who was very nearsighted and wore enormous, thick, convex lenses, went up to within a foot of the painting and, peering at it, said: 'I don't like this picture; you don't do Dr. Laws justice. You make him look like a goat.' Bingham, to whom the remarks had been addressed, replied sharply: 'Well, sir, you show yourself as much a judge of art as of propriety. This is a fine portrait of Dr. Laws, so acknowledged by the Doctor himself and his friends. Had I wanted to paint a goat, I should certainly have selected you for my model.' " [7]

Bingham's eminence as a man of affairs is made dramatic and alive by the Missouri historian who is the only remaining living man who knew the artist personally and intimately. "Bingham was a most versatile and talented man. To the gentle, delicate, refined attributes of the artist, he joined the strong, robust talents of the statesman and soldier. He was a charming correspondent and writer; yet he could, where a principle was involved, wield a dangerous and vitriolic pen. His character was invulnerable; no weak joint could be found in the armor of his pure and blameless life. And the man who sought a quarrel with Bingham, courted confusion. I think every public man who ever had a controversy with him would have agreed to this; they all emerged from the conflict badly maimed. Bingham was a fine conversationalist. It has always been a marvel to me where he got his pure English style and fund of information. The advantages of his early life had been meager indeed, but somehow, somewhere, sometime, he had read widely the best authors." [8]

The eulogistic phrases written by men who had known his life of public service were printed in the papers of Boonville, Independence, St. Louis, and Kansas City, and were reprinted in the news and periodicals which had nation-wide circulation.

The *Jefferson City People's Tribune*, July 16, 1879, quoted the following tribute from the *Kansas City Mail* of July 7: "General BINGHAM was in his 68th year, and no man was better known in Missouri either as an artist, as a powerful writer or a patriot of incorruptible integrity, always fearless and untiring in combating whatever he considered wrong. He had been respected in the councils of Missouri's foremost men for a generation past. His artistic labors have reflected lustre upon the taste and culture of the State. His record both as a citizen and as a public officer employed in trusts that test the purity of men, is one that the whole people may be proud of. His knightly spirit, always ready for the fray in the cause of justice and public morals, was unsubdued, and his brilliant mind was unclouded to the last. Dying at home in the bosom of the community he has served so long and so well, his old neighbors and friends will have the melancholy satisfaction of seeing that he is buried with the honors due to a citizen whose career has been so stainless and so eminent."

Bingham's sudden death arrested the growth of a personality whose very existence had been a dedication to his love for work. His large capacity for experience, his thirst for knowledge, his desire to set down in the midst of the tumult of exploration and settlement the scenes which everywhere he saw before him and which no painter would ever have the opportunity to witness again, his deep-seated yearning for honesty and honor in all his dealings bespeak him as a man who was made of that stuff, which, when it ceases to be, leaves a void so large that it can never quite be filled by the workers of a later day.

At the funeral services Major Rollins gave words to the respect that the state owed to her adopted son, and presented the tribute from those who loved him. Mr. C. B. Rollins has preserved an account of the memorial service which, written by one who heard Major Rollins, is the best reflection of what was said there: "Mr. Rollins is one of the most effective orators in the State, but the occasion, so solemn and impressive, and the presence of his dead friend before him, seemed to touch his lips with inspiration. His feelings chafing under the restraints of formal speech gave an eloquence that added to the richness of his imagery, and his words flowed out in chastened numbers that made his audience mourners with him. It was an occasion that brought out the finer shading of our better nature, and satisfied us with manhood and its nobler elements. It was a noble tribute by a manly man to a friend who could no longer speak for himself, and taught us the lesson that the most beautiful of all the gifts of our common father is true friendship among men. No mere report could do justice to this last tribute, for eloquent as were the words, beautiful as was the eulogy, the framework of the picture, the setting of the jewel was in the surroundings, the subdued manner of the speaker, the chastened cadence of his voice, the emphasis of heartfelt sorrow which no skill of the reporter could reproduce. Those who heard it will always carry with them a memory which is an event of a lifetime. It makes us think better of human nature, and teaches us that after all, men are better than we think." [9]

Because Bingham had, like a man who holds principles higher than comfort, stirred the anger of many and borne the hatred of a few during his active career, another paragraph must be added. "We do reverence to such men, whether we agree with their views of current, political and social questions or not. We look upon the men who fearlessly follow conscience and judgment in the abstract inquiring simply for right, for truth, for justice, as the noblest works of God on earth and whilst all such when we know them have our esteem and confidence they have our charity also. When, therefore, we differ from them as we did from Gen. Bingham quite recently, such difference abates not an iota of the feelings before entertained. A man without guile, whose courage was equal to the demands of duty, whose faith in the predominating power of truth never wavered, whose soul, so real, it could almost be seen with human eyes, was George C. Bingham. The mysterious link that bound such a being to mortality, was easily rent as smoking flax dropping away the frail tenement as a worn out useless thing, the soul springing as we fondly believe into an eternity of perfected life and infinite duty. Thou hast triumphed at last, friend Bingham!" [10]

In his *Recollections*, Mr. C. B. Rollins wrote this tribute to his father's most intimate friend: "Certainly if I were called upon to name six of the most noted men in the history of the state, near the top of the list I would place the name of George Caleb Bingham."

The Bingham Revival: An Evaluation

A UNIQUE parallelism in the history of American art lies in the fact that both George Caleb Bingham and Thomas Hart Benton have grounded their roots deep in the soil of Missouri. Though separated in time by nearly half a century, they are bound together by a kinship in spirit that is timeless. The nineteenth century artist depicted honestly the view directly before him; Benton, more and more, pictures realistically the scene in his native state as he sees it today. And both are believed by many competent critics to rear, head and shoulders, above most of their contemporaries who might be attracted by, and working with, the art of everyday life.[1] The one was a pioneer; the other is a titanic developer.

"It is somehow extraordinary to realize," wrote Marquis W. Childs as late as 1934, "that the Middlewest had a painter of some stature as early as 1850. . . . For the first time a serious effort has been made to assemble a representative collection of the work of this forgotten American painter."[2]

The St. Louis exhibit to which he referred was not, however, the first "serious effort" made to show a representative group of Bingham's works. The Missouri painter had not been altogether "forgotten." From the ninth of April to the twenty-fourth, 1910, the Art Lovers' Guild of Columbia, Missouri, presented a special exhibition of paintings by Bingham, in the Museum of Classical Archeology of the University of Missouri. Those were not lacking who, through the years, had kept the candles burning at the Bingham shrine. Most of these loyal enthusiasts were Missourians, some of them interested in art itself, but others more enthusiastic about Missouriana in general. So, sectionally at least, Bingham was remembered and paid honor.

A trio of women seem to have been the first who set out to collect material concerning the artist, though their findings were never bound into book form.[3] Today's Bingham enthusiasts may be thankful for the material that was preserved by these devoted friends of the artist.

In 1914 Miss Fern Helen Rusk collected an astounding number of facts, and recounted them in 1917 in an excellent volume of one hundred and thirty-five pages, with a few illustrations.

It was not until April of 1934, however, that Bingham was "dusted off and cleaned up."[4] At that time the City Art Museum of St. Louis exhibited twenty paintings and eight prints. Assisted by the man who has been most interested to see a healthy Bingham "revival," Mr. C. B. Rollins, Columbia, Meyric R. Rogers, director of the museum, gave the Middlewest its first widely publicized showing of its earliest artist of note. The collection was, in the same year, shown in the William Rockhill Nelson Gallery in Kansas City. Then, in the spring of 1935, the canvases and prints were shown in the Museum of Modern Art, New York. And, finally, the exhibit was presented to New England at Hartford, Connecticut. This was, one might say, the "official" debut of Bingham into the modern art world.

Now, it seems reasonable to ask, what are the living qualities that revived the Missouri artist; must we not be suspicious of the recently resurrected life, in light of the fact that there has been a general tendency to acclaim all things American in our art? Is Bingham real, or is he riding on this wave of the sometimes uncritical popularity of Americanism, regionalism and localism.[5]

Bingham's fame must rest upon merit. A momentary revival, based only upon a flighty infatuation with yesterday's Americanisms, will serve but to send the artist into eventual oblivion. What, of his work, has this merit? Where and what is it?

The portraits, the historical scenes, and the genre work treated here probably represent that work upon which a claim for Bingham's immortality must rest. It is the work which has been selected by that only certain critic—Time.

There is sincerity in this work. When these pictures are studied, the truth, for which Bingham had such love, is made known. And, as was written twenty years ago, before the absorption in the "revival" might have vitiated judgment, it is "because of this sincere, truthful interpretation and portrayal of the life of his time in Missouri," that "Bingham's work stands at the head of American genre painting in the second quarter of the nineteenth century, and it is upon these worth-while characteristics that his claim to future recognition is based." [6] Today's renewed interest is the "future recognition" which was prophesied by Miss Rusk in 1914.

Matthew Arnold accused the Wordsworthians of admiring their poet for the wrong qualities. In attempting to appraise Bingham's work we shall do him small service by reading into his paintings currently fashionable qualities whether or not they are there. Though we may seem excessively modest in the merits we ascribe to him, we feel that such modesty is fairer to his reputation than the meretricious glamour of popularity. When we judge a minor artist by the same standards as those by which we judge the greatest, we are not likely to flatter him, but we are reasonably certain to discover the truth.

The Chronology

1811 March 20. Born on a plantation on South River, Augusta County, Virginia.

1819 Family moved to Franklin, Missouri.

1823 December 26. Father died.

1824 Mother opened school for girls at Franklin.

1827 April 19. Farm near Arrow Rock secured for Mrs. Bingham by members of Masonic Order of Franklin.

1827 Tutored by Jesse Green, cabinetmaker and Methodist minister near Arrow Rock.

1827–8 Apprenticed to Justinian Williams, cabinetmaker and Methodist minister in Franklin.

1827–30 Studied religion, preached, and read law.

1830 Professionally engaged painting portraits.

1830 Attempted trip to St. Louis. Fell seriously ill on the way, and was forced to return home.

1830–4 Became an itinerant portrait painter.

1834 Visited Columbia, where he met James S. Rollins and painted his portrait.

1835 Painted *Self Portrait.*

1835 December (probably). Arrived in St. Louis.

1836 April. Married Miss Elizabeth Hutchison.

1837 May 6, from Natchez. Wrote his first known letter to his friend, Major James S. Rollins.

1837 May 27. Returned to Boonville.

1837 Spent summer in Columbia, painting portraits.

1837 In the fall went to Philadelphia where he studied three months in the Academy of Fine Arts.

1838 Visited New York City during early months of the year.

1838 Returned to Arrow Rock later in the year and painted portraits.

1838–40 Began to sketch panorama of Missouri life in the country and along the River.

1840 Became involved in politics; spoke at the Rocheport Whig Convention. Sketched at these political meetings.

1840	Went to Washington, D. C., where he was, in the main, occupied with portrait painting during the following four years. During these four years he spent six months in Petersburg, Virginia.
1844	In Washington he completed his first known genre picture: *Jolly Flatboatmen*.
1845	Registered with American Art Union from St. Louis.
1846	June 24. Was nominated Whig candidate for State Legislature from Saline County.
1846	Completed: *Boatmen on Missouri; Landscape with Cattle*.
1846	August 14. Elected to State Legislature.
1846	November 20. E. D. Sappington, his opponent, contested his election.
1846	December 18. Case won by Sappington.
1847	Registered in the American Art Union from Arrow Rock.
1847	Completed: *Lighter Relieving a Steamboat Aground; Raftsmen Playing Cards; Old Field Horse; Lumbermen Dining; The Horse Thief*.
1848	Completed: *Captured by Indians* (?); *Stump Orator; Portrait of Oscar F. Potter*.
1848	May 1. Declined nomination as Representative in State Legislature from Saline County.
1848	July 7. Accepted the nomination.
1848	August 1. Elected to State House of Representatives.
1848	November 29. Wife died in Arrow Rock, Missouri.
1849	Completed: *County Politician; St. Louis Wharf; Woodyard; A Boatman; Raftsmen on the Ohio; Watching the Cargo*.
1849	February 26. As member of the Committee on Federal Relations in the State Legislature, he reported the decision of that body upon the subjects of slavery and of secession.
1849	August and September. Visited in New York City, where he displayed work.
1849	September 28. At portrait work in Columbia.
1849	December 2. Married Miss Eliza Thomas of Columbia.
1850	Worked in St. Louis. Exhibited *Shooting for the Beef*.
1850–51	Completed: *Cattle Piece; Fishing on the Mississippi* (or Missouri?); *The Squatters; The Wood Boat; Trapper's Return; Chess Players*.
1850–51	In New York.
1851	At work on *The Emigration of Boone*.
1851	May 23. Stopped in St. Louis on way home from New York.

1851	By summer, returned to Columbia where he opened a studio.
1851	October 31. Exhibited in Columbia studio: *County Election; Canvassing for a Vote; Landscape Scene on the Ohio; Chess Players.*
1851	November 24. In St. Louis and planned to paint portraits throughout the winter.
1852	Completed: *Belated Wayfarers* (?).
1852	March 19. Still in St. Louis. Sold subscriptions for *County Election* prints.
1852	April 2. Visited Columbia and exhibited *County Election.*
1852	June 3. Went to Baltimore, where he spent some days as delegate to the Whig National Convention.
1852	June 27. In Philadelphia where he made arrangements with Sartain for engraving *County Election.* Engraving of *Raftsmen Playing Cards* by Goupil & Company finished and prints made.
1852	November 21. Visited St. Louis.
1853	March 10. Left for New Orleans where he exhibited *County Election.*
1853	May 22 and July 5. Wrote to Rollins from Lexington, Kentucky, where he was seeking subscriptions for prints of *County Election.*
1853	September. Visited New York.
1853	October 3. In Philadelphia supervising the work of engraving the plate of *County Election.*
1853	November. Began *Stump Speaking (County Canvass).*
1853	November 23. Believed he would finish *Stump Speaking* by January.
1853	December 12. Described *Stump Speaking* in a letter to Rollins.
1854	February 1. Incensed with Sartain's delay in engraving *County Election* plate.
1854	April 6. Sold copyrights of *Stump Speaking* to Goupil & Company; conceived the idea of the *Verdict of the People.*
1854	May 17. Visited in New York. Worked on studies for *The Verdict of the People.*
1854	May 29 and July 15. In Philadelphia.
1854	September 15. Returned to St. Louis for a time. Went back to the east probably in the next year.
1855	Supposedly left Philadelphia in the spring.
1855	June 21. Wrote to Rollins from Independence, Missouri, that *Verdict of the People* had been completed before he left Philadelphia.
1855	September 14. Painted portraits in his studio in the Grand Jury room of the courthouse, Columbia.

1855	November 14. Painted portraits in his studio in the Capitol, Jefferson City.
1855	December 14. Spoke recently at a Whig meeting at Jefferson City.
1856	March 14. Worked upon the historical painting, *Washington Crossing the Delaware.*
1856	May 16. In St. Louis, with exhibition of *Verdict of the People.*
1856	June 2. Wrote to Rollins of the success of *Verdict of the People.* Planned to leave for Philadelphia and go from there to Boston to copy heads of Washington and Jefferson for Missouri Capitol pictures, contracted for recently.
1856	June 29. Arrived in Boston and copied Stuart's portraits of Washington and Jefferson.
1856	June–July. Returned to Philadelphia.
1856	August 10. Wrote to Rollins from Philadelphia.
1856	August 14. Embarked on Steam Ship *Vigo* for Havre.
1856	September 7. Wrote to his friend from Paris, where he studied in the Louvre. He spent several months in the city.
1856	November 4. In Düsseldorf.
1856	December 14. Worked on full-length portrait of Washington.
1857	June 3. Planned to complete portraits of Washington and Jefferson during summer. Arranged for publishing *Verdict of the People.* Worked also on *Jolly Flatboatmen* (No. 3).
1857	October 12. *Jolly Flatboatmen* near completion.
1857	*The First Music Lesson* was on exhibit in the Pennsylvania Academy of Fine Arts.
1858	March 8. Still in Düsseldorf.
1859	January 28. Returned to Jefferson City with the portraits of Washington and Jefferson.
1859	January 29. Visited Major Rollins in Columbia.
1859	February 19. Wrote from St. Louis that he was highly honored to receive commission to paint portraits of Jackson and Clay.
1859	Painted the portrait of Dr. Troost of Kansas City.
1859	April 22. Painted portraits in Brunswick.
1859	May 1–17. Commissioned by the Mercantile Library Association, St. Louis, to paint a portrait of Baron von Humboldt.
1859	May 13. Left Columbia for Düsseldorf.
1859	June 6. Wrote Rollins from Düsseldorf that von Humboldt had recently died.

1859	September 9. Returned to Columbia because of the death of his father-in-law.
1859–60	Went east for a time, probably to study the head of Jackson by Sully.
1860	February 24. Returned to Columbia.
1860	April 27. Von Humboldt portrait delivered to the Mercantile Library.
1860	September 15. Wrote to Rollins from Independence, Missouri, that the Jackson portrait was completed.
1860	November 27. In Kansas City. Planned to finish the Clay portrait within three weeks.
1861	January 12. In Jefferson City. Wrote to Rollins that the portraits of Clay and Jackson had been placed in the Hall of Representatives (January 8).
1861	March 6. Distressed over the political and social outlook.
1861	June 5. Wrote to his friend from Kansas City that there was no portrait work to be obtained.
1861	In the summer he was appointed captain in the United States Reserve Corps, in Kansas City.
1861	June 29. Wrote to Rollins stating that the position was not pleasant for him.
1862	January 4. Resigned captaincy in Kansas City and was appointed State Treasurer.
1862	August 1. Agreed to paint an equestrian portrait of General Lyon.
1862	August 13. Wrote to his sister concerning his position in regard to the war.
1863	August 25. "General Order No. 11" was issued by General Ewing.
1863	December 21. Has become very fatigued with position of Treasurer.
1865	The term of office as Treasurer expired.
1865	November 14. Resided at Independence, Missouri, and painted *Order No. 11*.
1866	June 1. Became candidate for Congress from the Sixth District.
1866	July 6. At work painting *Major Dean in Jail*.
1866	October 6. Was defeated as candidate for Congress in the nominating convention.
1867	July 10. Wrote to Rollins concerning his attitude toward the "enemy."
1868	May 28. Election at the Democratic State Convention.

1868	December 11. Completed *Order No. 11*.
1869	March 17. Defended his polemic picture in an open letter.
1869	October 1. Was elected a school director in Independence, Missouri.
1870	May 6. Sold his home in Independence and moved to Kansas City.
1871	May 5. Completed the portrait of General Frank P. Blair.
1871	June 19. Wrote to his friend from Kansas City concerning art.
1871	In the fall of that year a group of friends of Major Rollins asked the artist to paint a portrait of his friend.
1871	December 24. In Philadelphia, supervising the engraving of the plate, *Order No. 11*.
1872	January 7. Wrote that Sartain was eager to engrave a plate from *Washington Crossing the Delaware*.
1872	January 17. Sartain was slow to complete the engraving, *Order No. 11*.
1872	May 10. In Kansas City. Reported to Rollins that the prints of *Order No. 11* were popular.
1872	During the summer the artist and his wife made a trip to Colorado.
1872	October 26. A communication from Denver described the canvas, *View of Pike's Peak*.
1872	November 20. In Kansas City.
1873	March 24. Completed portrait of Major James S. Rollins.
1873	May 2. In Texas.
1873	August 3. Wrote his appreciation for tribute paid him by the Board of Curators of the University of Missouri.
1873	September 3. In Columbia. Paid a visit to his friend, planned to leave shortly for Louisville, Kentucky.
1874	May 11. Appointed president of the Kansas City Board of Police Commissioners.
1874	July 31. Accepted candidacy for Congress from the Eighth District.
1874	August 24. Declined the candidacy.
1874	December 11. *The Puzzled Witness* was exhibited in St. Louis.
1875	January. Received the appointment of Adjutant-General from Governor Charles H. Hardin.
1875	January 19. Took up the duties of his new office.
1876	February 23. In Washington, D. C., on state business.
1876	April 13. Began portrait of Vinnie Ream.
1876	May 1. Returned from Washington.

1876	October 15. Revealed to his friend, in a letter from Kansas City, that his wife had become mentally deranged.
1876	October 24. Given indefinite leave from the state office because of his ill health.
1876	November 3. Wife died in the asylum at Fulton, Missouri.
1876	December 14. Had grown discouraged with the Treasurer's position.
1877	January 19. Appointed professor of art at the University of Missouri.
1877	September 9. Wrote to Rollins regarding the teaching position.
1877	November 4. Wrote from Kansas City and expressed the desire to be a member of the delegation representing the United States at the Paris Exposition.
1878	June 18. Married his third wife, Mrs. Mattie Lykins of Kansas City.
1878	November 3. Was appointed commissioner to select a design for the Robert E. Lee Monument Association of the State of Virginia.
1878	November 21. Arrived in Richmond, Virginia.
1878	December 6. Returned to Columbia from the east. Roomed at Stephens College.
1879	February 28. Was seriously ill with pneumonia.
1879	March 1. His friend, Major Rollins, reads Bingham's written address upon art in the University Chapel.
1879	May 5. Wrote to his friend, assuring Rollins that he had fully recovered his health.
1879	June 13. Published an attack upon Ewing's *Order No. 11*.
1879	June 17. Was given a reply by Ex-Governor B. Gratz Brown.
1879	July 7. Died suddenly after an attack of cholera morbus.

Selected Bibliography

Books

Bingham, G. C. "Art, the Ideal of Art and the Utility of Art," University of Missouri *Public Lectures*, 1878–79, Course II, Vol. I. Columbia: Statesman Book and Job Print, 1879.

Brashear, Minnie M. *Mark Twain, Son of Missouri*. Chapel Hill: The University of North Carolina Press, 1934, pp. 37–48.

Chalkley, Lyman. *Chronicles of the Scotch Irish Settlement in Virginia*, extracted from the original Court Records of Augusta County, 1745–1800. Rosslyn, Va.: Published by Mary S. Lockwood. Printers: The Commonwealth Company, II–III.

Conrad, Howard Lewis, ed. *Encyclopedia of the History of Missouri*. New York, Louisville (etc.): The Southern History Company, Haldeman, Conrad and Company, proprietors, 1901, VIII, 310 ff.

Crittenden, H. H. *The Crittenden Memoirs*. New York: G. P. Putnam's Sons, 1936, p. 342.

Denslow, Ray V. *A Missouri Frontier Lodge*, the Story of Franklin Union Lodge No. 7 at Old Franklin, Missouri, 1822–32. Published by the Masonic Service Association of Missouri, 1929.

Dictionary of American Biography, edited by Allen Johnson and Dumas Malone. New York: Charles Scribner's Sons, 1931, III, 597–598.

History of Saline County, Missouri, St. Louis: Missouri Historical Company, 1881, p. 174.

Missouri, Laws of, First General Assembly, First Session, 1820, Section 13, pp. 18–21.

Rusk, Fern Helen. *George Caleb Bingham, The Missouri Artist*. Jefferson City: The Hugh Stephens Company, 1917.

Smith, W. B. *James Sidney Rollins*. New York: De Vinne Press, 1891.

Spraker, Hazel A. *The Boone Family*. Rutland, Vermont: The Tuttle Company, 1922, pp. 568, 578–579.

Switzler. *History of Missouri*, St. Louis: C. R. Barnes, Editor and Publisher, 1879, p. 256.

Thwaites, R. G. "S. H. Long's Expedition." *Early Western Travels*, Cleveland: The Arthur H. Clark Company, XIV, 148–157.

Trusler, Rev. John. *The Works of William Hogarth*. London and New York: The London Printing and Publishing Company, I.

Viles, Jonas. *A History of Missouri*. New York: The MacMillan Company, 1935, p. 236.

Newspapers

Boonville Observer, October 15, 1844, June 24, 1846, March 11, 1847.

Boonville (Missouri) Weekly Advertiser, June 14, 1901.

Boonville Weekly Eagle, October 12, 1877.

Columbia Statesman, August 31, 1849, December 12, 27, 1850.

Glasgow Weekly Times, November 23, 1854.

Jefferson City Daily Tribune, March 4, 1876, from the *Saline County Progress*.

Jefferson City Inquirer, February 5, 1859, January 12, 1861.

Jefferson City Metropolitan, August 17, 1847.

Jefferson City People's Tribune, July 16, 1819, January 25, 1871.

Jeffersonian Republican, January 2, 1836.

Jefferson City Tribune, June 20, 1878.

Jefferson City Weekly People's Tribune, December 23, 1868.

Missouri Intelligencer & Boon's Lick Advertiser, Columbia, June 28, 1834, March 14, 1835.

Missouri Statesman, December 29, 1848, December 7, 1849, October 31, 1851, January 1, 1869.

Sentinal-Tribune, Kansas City, July 10, 1879.

St. Louis Missouri Republican, April 17, 1849, March 17, 1869.

St. Louis Republican, November 28, 1847.

Periodicals

Childs, Marquis W., "George Caleb Bingham," *American Magazine of Art*, XXVII (November, 1934), 594–599.

Culmer, Frederic A., "Abiel Leonard," *The Missouri Historical Review*, XXVII, No. 2 (January, 1933), 113–131.

The Missouri Historical Review, XXV, No. 4 (July, 1931), 636; XVIII, No. 2 (January, 1934), 130–133; XXX, No. 4 (July, 1936), 468.

Morsell, Mary, "Modern Museum Holds Exhibition of Bingham's Art," *The Art News*, February 2, 1935, p. 6.

The Museum of Modern Art, *George Caleb Bingham, The Missouri Artist, 1811–1879*, New York, (January 30–March 7) 1935.

Musick, James B., "Bingham's Historical Background in Missouri," *George Caleb Bingham, the Missouri Artist, 1811–1879*, pp. 13–14.

Pope, Arthur, "Bingham's Technique and Composition," *George Caleb Bingham, The Missouri Artist, 1811–1879*, pp. 15–16.

Rogers, Meyric R., *Bulletin of the City Art Museum of St. Louis*, XIX, No. 2 (April, 1934), 14–24.

Rogers, Meyric R., "George Caleb Bingham, 1811–1879," *George Caleb Bingham, the Missouri Artist, 1811–1879*, pp. 7–12.

Rollins, C. B., "Some Recollections of George Caleb Bingham," *The Missouri Historical Review*, XX, No. 4 (July, 1926), 463–484.

Viles, Jonas, "Old Franklin: A Frontier Town of the Twenties," *The Mississippi Valley Historical Review*, IX, No. 4 (March, 1923), 269.

Letters

The letters from George Caleb Bingham to Major James Sidney Rollins may be found in the files of the State Historical Society of Missouri, University Library, Columbia, Missouri. Because the writer has obtained the excerpts used in this volume from copies of the original letters, he cannot guarantee their strict accuracy. However, special care was exercised in reproducing these letters; the individualistic spelling and the uniqueness of some of the grammatical constructions are Bingham's.

Notes

HISTORICAL BACKGROUND IN MISSOURI

1. Musick, "Bingham's Historical Background in Missouri," *George Caleb Bingham, The Missouri Artist, 1811–1879*, p. 18.

2. Viles, "Old Franklin: A Frontier Town of the Twenties," *The Mississippi Valley Historical Review*, IX, No. 4 (March, 1923), 269.

3. Irving had written back to his sister: "Our journey has been a very interesting one, leading us across fine prairies and through noble forests, dotted here and there by farms and log houses, at which we found rough but wholesome fare, and very civil treatment. Many parts of these prairies of the Missouri are extremely beautiful, resembling cultivated countries embellished with parks and groves, rather than the savage rudeness of the wilderness. . . . The fertility of this western country is truly astonishing. The soil is like that of a garden, and the luxuriance and beauty of the forest exceed anything I have ever seen. We have gradually been advancing, however, toward rougher and rougher life, and are now at a little straggling frontier village that has only been five years in existence. . . ." *Life and Letters of Irving*, I, 248.

4. Thwaites, "S. H. Long's Expedition," *Early Western Travels*, XIV, 148.

5. Conard, *Encyclopedia of the History of Missouri*, III, 310 ff.

6. "Sec. 13.

"That an academy be, and the same is hereby established at the Town of Franklin, in the County of Howard, which shall be called and known by the name of Franklin Academy; that

> Thomas B. Smith
> N. Hutchison
> John J. Lowry
> Geo. Tompkins
> James C. Ludlow
> Taylor Berry
> Jonathan S. Findlay

be a body politic and corporate, to be known by the name of the Trustees of the Franklin Academy. Nov. 16, 1820."
—*Laws of Missouri*, 1st General Assembly, 1st Session (1820), Sec. 13, pp. 18–21.

7. Denslow, Ray V., "Who's Who of Franklin Union Lodge," *A Missouri Frontier Lodge, the Story of Franklin Union Lodge No. 7 at Old Franklin, Missouri*, p. 88.

8. *"Notice*

Gentlemen who have *Books* belonging to the *Franklin Library Company*, will please to return them, as the business of the library cannot be carried on unless the rules are observed.

John J. Lowry, Librarian"

"Franklin, Nov. 12"

—*The Missouri Historical Review*, XXV, No. 4 (July, 1931), 636, taken from the *Missouri Intelligencer and Boon's Lick Advertiser*, Franklin, November 12, 1819.

9. *The Missouri Historical Review*, XXVI, No. 1 (October, 1931), p. 94.

10. Culmer, "Abiel Leonard," *The Missouri Historical Review*, XXVII, No. 2 (January, 1933), 113–131.

11. "First Printing Press West of St. Louis

"The Mercantile Library Association of this city now have in their possession the second printing press ever west of the Mississippi and the first ever west of St. Louis. It is a small wooden machine, iron leed, of the old Ramage pattern; and notwithstanding its age is still in working order. It is a present to the Association from Co. Switzler of the Columbia (Mo.) *Statesman*, and can be seen in their hall with this placard upon it:

" 'Presented to the Mercantile Library Association by Wm. F. Switzler, editor of the *Missouri Statesman*, Columbia, Mo., May, 1864. This press is the same one which Nathaniel Patton printed the *Missouri Intelligencer* in Franklin, Howard county, Mo., in 1819; is the second printing press ever West of the Mississippi and the first ever west of St. Louis.' "

—*The Missouri Historical Review*, XXX, No. 4 (July, 1936), 468, taken from the St. Louis *Tri-Weekly Missouri Republican*, June 22, 1864.

12. "But what of John Hardeman, himself, whom Senator Benton characterized as 'a gentleman of science, character, and fortune, greatly attached to the pursuits of agriculture'? Strange tales were told about Hardeman, and because so little was known about him, many of them were believed. But most of them are untrue.

"It was said that Hardeman was of German origin, that he had written a book in German, and that he had been a south sea pirate, but these stories were denied by one of his grand-daughters. According to the late Miss Julia Dunnica of Glasgow, grand-daughter of John Hardeman, he was born in America in 1776, and was of English descent. Miss Dunnica did not say where Hardeman was born, but one account indicates that he was a native of North Carolina.

"That Hardeman and his family lived at one time in Tennessee is almost certain, for the letter mentioned above makes an allusion to one of his sons, John Locke Hardeman, was born in that State on July 27, 1809. Apparently the family moved to Missouri in 1819, settling in the famed Boon's Lick country, where John Hardeman developed his remarkable botanical garden.

"That John Hardeman was a man of wealth, refinement and culture is affirmed by nearly all sources. The fact that he purchased a large tract of land in Howard county would indicate that he was a man of some wealth. He is claimed to have been a graduate of Princeton University, although the University records do not verify this statement. The nature and extent of his agricultural experiments certainly indicate a man of scientific inclinations, while the letter cited above shows that he must indeed have been a man of considerably more education than the average of his time and locality."—*The Missouri Historical Review*, XXVIII, No. 2 (January, 1934), 130–133.

13. "Probably the first of the pioneer physicians to settle in that section of the country, known as Old Franklin, was Dr. Hardage Lane. He was a cousin of Dr. William Carr Lane of St. Louis, and was regarded by the people of this age as one of the most accomplished of his profession in the state. His practice at the active period of his life was not only large but lucrative and embraced the best families of St. Louis, where he later resided. His entire attention was given to the practice of medicine and to his Masonic duties, so that he was less conspicuous in political circles and not generally known as was his cousin, Mayor Lane. . . . His wife preceded him in death three years, having died on August 17th, 1846, in her forty-third year; she was Miss Anne Carroll, a daughter of Charles Carroll of New York, who was killed in the Gentry duel. He was a very hospitable man and entertained a great deal of company; his wife was an accomplished woman and a leader in society; and the elegant dinners and fashionable parties given at the Lane home were the talk of the city."—Denslow, *A Missouri Frontier Lodge, the Story of Franklin Union Lodge No. 7 at Old Franklin, Missouri*, p. 65.

14. The writer is obligated to Mr. Roy King, of the State Historical Society of Missouri, for the information gleaned through patient research, revealing the character of a person of exciting interest, Josiah Gregg.

15. "Josiah Gregg, in his rare volume 'Commerce of the Prairies,' published in 1844, speaks of the town of Old Franklin:

" 'People who reside at a distance, and especially at the north have generally considered St. Louis as the Emporium of the Santa Fe trade, but that city, in truth, has never been a place of rendezvous, or even of outfit, except for a small portion of the traders who have started from its immediate vicinity.

" 'The town of Franklin (founded in 1816 on the north bank of the Missouri river, opposite the impending town of Boonville) about one hundred fifty miles farther to the westward, seems largely to have been the cradle of our trade: and in conjunction with several neighboring towns, continued, for many years, to furnish the greater number of these adventureous traders. Even subsequently to 1831 many wagons have been fitted out and started from this interior section. But as the navigation of the Missouri river had been considerable advanced towards the year 1831, and the advantages of some point of debarkation nearer the western frontier were very evident, whereby upwards of a hundred miles of troublesome land-carriage over unimproved and often miry roads might be avoided, the new town of Independence, but twelve miles from the Indian border and two or three south of the

Missouri river being the most eligible point, soon began to take the lead as a place of debarkation, outfit, and departure.' "—Denslow, *op. cit.*, p. 5.

16. Denslow, "Who's Who of Franklin Union Lodge," *op. cit.*, pp. 85–98.

17. *Ibid.*, p. 85.

18. *Ibid.*, p. 97.

19. Rollins, "Some Recollections of George Caleb Bingham," *The Missouri Historical Review*, p. 471.

20. See p. 8.

21. See p. 13.

22. Brashear, *op. cit.*, p. 48.

23. "Now that his work has been dusted off and cleaned up, it is difficult to understand why this painter was so long neglected. For it would seem that merely as a record of a peculiarly fascinating phase of his past work it should have held attention. But perhaps it was necessary to be removed from that phase by a certain number of decades before this was apparent. And possibly a shift in taste had to occur that we might outgrow a prejudice against paintings that seemed 'old fashioned.'

"The Bingham exhibit, along with the re-discovery of Currier and Ives and the rise of such painters as Grant Wood and John Steuart Curry, seems tangible proof of a new trend. Painting that is laboratory painting, experimental painting, too often static, no longer holds the entire stage. We look with interest suddenly renewed at these big canvases crowded with figures in attitudes familiar and yet strange, glowing with a life that is common and yet remote and unknown."—Childs, "George Caleb Bingham," *American Magazine of Art*, XXVII (November, 1934), p. 595.

24. See p. 13.

25. Included in Long's Expedition, which stopped at Old Franklin for six days in 1819, we find the names of Peale and Seymour.

According to a footnote supplementing the account of the expedition, "Titian Ramsey Peale (1800–1885) came of a family which has produced a remarkable number of artists, the most notable being a brother, Rembrandt. His father, an uncle, another brother, and three cousins achieved more or less distinction in that field. Like his father and brother, T. R. Peale divided his attention between art and natural science. He was an officer of the Philadelphia Academy, and author of *Mammalia and Ornithology* (1848). From 1838 to 1842 he was a member of Lieutenant Charles Wilkes's exploring expedition to the South Sea; during the years 1849–72 he was an examiner in the patent office.

"The events of the life of Samuel Seymour are now not known."

The official duties of the two men were described in the expedition records: "Mr. Peale will officiate as assistant naturalist. In the several departments above enumerated, his services will be required in collecting specimans suitable to be preserved, in drafting and delineating them, in preserving the skins, etc. of animals, and in sketching the stratifications of rocks, earths, etc. as presented on the declivities of precipices.

"Mr. Seymour, as painter for the expedition will furnish sketches of landscapes, whenever we meet with any distinguished for their beauty and grandeur. He will also paint miniature likenesses, or portraits, if required, of distinguished Indians, and exhibit groups of savages engaged in celebrating their festivals, or sitting in council, and in general illustrate any subject, that may be deemed appropriate in his art."—Thwaites, "S. H. Long's Expedition," *Early Western Travels*, XIV, 40–43.

26. See pp. 17 and 18.

27. Brashear, *op. cit.*, p. 254.

28. Brashear, *op. cit.*, p. 263.

THE HERITAGE

1. "Recorded in Rockingham County is a deed dated Dec. 9, 1809, from Nathias Amond of that county to Henry V. Bingham of 1180 acres on South River, and also on the same date, Nathias Amond deeded 10¾ acres in Rockingham County to Henry V. Bingham."—Augusta County *Court Records*, II, 265. (The writer is indebted for this information to Mr. R. A. Lancaster, Jr., Corresponding Secretary of the Virginia Historical Society.)

2. From a copy by Miss May Simonds of the original manuscript, owned by Rollins Bingham in 1902.

3. In the abstracts from *Records of Augusta County, Virginia*, "Bingham" is sometimes spelled "Bingaman."

4. Rusk, *op. cit.*, p. 7. From Mrs. Louise J. Bingham Neff's unpublished "Sketch of Bingham."

THE EARLY LIFE

1. Conard, *Encyclopedia of the History of Missouri*, III, 310 ff.

2. *Bulletin* of the American Art Union, August, 1849, pp. 10–12.

3. Pope, "Bingham's Technique and Composition," *George Caleb Bingham, The Missouri Artist, 1811–1879*, p. 15.

4. See p. 13.

5. See p. 11.

6. Conard, *op. cit.*, III, 310 ff.

7. Neff, Mrs. L. J. B., unpublished "Sketch of Bingham."

8. See p. 6.

9. Spraker, *The Boone Family*, pp. 578–579.

10. Also, according to Spraker (p. 567), Daniel Boone was father of only ten children, one of whom died in infancy, and not eighteen as represented by Miss Rusk to be stated in Harding's *My Egotistography*. It is possible that Boone's grand-children were present at the painting of the portrait and might have increased the

number of onlookers to eighteen, as Harding states.

11. Rusk, *op. cit.*, p. 16.

12. Denslow, *op. cit.*, p. 18.

13. The date of the moving is 1823 in Rusk's account. This supposition on her part is no doubt incorrect, because H. V. Bingham died on December 26 of that year. It seems highly improbable that the family would have left Franklin within three days after the death of the father.

14. Rollins, *op. cit.*, p. 471.

15. *History of Saline County*, p. 174.

16. See note 19 on "Historical Background in Missouri."

17. Rollins, C. B.

18. See p. 33.

19. Rollins, *op. cit.*, p. 482.

20. *Ibid.*, p. 482.

21. Rusk, *op. cit.*, pp. 20–21.

22. Rollins, *op. cit.*, p. 464.

23. *Missouri Statesman*, August 15, 1879.

24. *Columbia Statesman*, August 31, 1849.

25. *Boonville Missouri Advertiser*, June 14, 1901.

THE EARLY WORK

1. This article, according to Mr. C. B. Rollins, was undoubtedly written by Pres. Thomas Miller, Columbia College.

2. Rusk, *op. cit.*, p. 19.

3. ". . . the young man spent one year in caring for the large farm of his father, two years in the private study of the law in the office of Abiel Leonard, afterwards a Supreme Court Judge of Missouri, and then, returning to Kentucky, he completed the law course at Transylvania, Lexington, graduating in the spring of 1834 at the age of twenty-two."—Smith, *James Sidney Rollins*, p. 5.

4. *Ibid.*

5. This is the earliest portrait of any quality which is known today. Fern Helen Rusk says: "A portrait of Judge David Todd, a lawyer who settled in Franklin in the early days, is reckoned as our artist's first serious work. (She obtained her evidence from the *Missouri Statesman*, January 16, 1880.) The painting was destroyed in the University of Missouri fire of 1892; but a photograph of it shows us the general character of the work."—pp. 18–19. Now Bingham did, certainly, paint a portrait of Todd; but the photograph to which Miss Rusk refers is a likeness of a copy of Bingham's portrait of the lawyer, executed by an unknown St. Louis artist. This painting now hangs in the County Court House, Columbia, Missouri. Mr. N. T. Gentry, lawyer, descendant of Todd, agrees to the truth of this statement. There is a serious question, also, as to the authenticity of the portrait of Mrs. Wm. John-

ston (Plate III in Rusk), says Mr. Rollins.

6. "*James S. Rollins*, Attorney at Law,

"Having settled permanently in Columbia, respectfully tenders his professional services to the citizens of Boone, Howard, Callaway and Monroe counties. His office is the new brick building, on the east side of Guitar Street, where he will at all times give the most prompt attention to the duties of his profession. Columbia, April, 1834."—*Missouri Intelligencer & Boon's Lick Advertiser*, June 28, 1834.

7. Childs, *op. cit.*, p. 596.

8. "Both men were voluminous writers, and at least a thousand letters must have passed between them."—Rollins, *op. cit.*, p. 463.

9. Excerpts from the letters contained in this volume were taken from copies of the original letters now in the manuscript collection of the State Historical Society of Missouri, Columbia. The complete letters have been published since in the *Missouri Historical Review*.

10. "As I look at that full-length portrait of the esteemed President of the Board, painted by one whom I am proud to call my personal friend and professional brother, George C. Bingham, I am reminded of the fact that both the subject of this picture and the artist have been, from early youth to manhood's ripened years, the warmest personal friends, and, next to his own kith and kin, each has by the other been best beloved.

"Together they have traveled life's pathway; side by side have they labored; contributing in the Legislature and out of it, as best they might, all the power of their united personal influence to promote the best interests of this great commonwealth.

"In political action, they have been one; and in sentiment and affection like David and Jonathan, they have been united by ties most intimate and tender.

"This portrait of the founder of this University, painted by the father of Missouri art, and crowning work of his life in the line of portraiture—whose fame rests not alone upon this branch, for he has given to posterity those inimitable delineations of human character as presented in the history of the early political life of Missouri in those well known election scenes—this portrait, I say, to us who are gathered here today, has not alone the interest of being a worthy tribute to a worthy man, but around it cluster the memories of the hard-fought battles of civil and political conflict and the tender associations of undying friendship."—Smith, *op. cit.*, p. 303.

11. Rollins, *op. cit.*, p. 463.

12. Smith, *op. cit.*, p. 73.

13. These articles made available through the courtesy of Mr. Roy King, State Historical Society of Missouri.

14. Smith, *op. cit.*, pp. 72–73.

THE ADVENTURE

1. See p. 17.

2. Rusk, *op. cit.*, p. 21, quoting from Miss May Simonds' unpublished "Sketch of Bingham's Life."

3. *Ibid.*, p. 22, quoting from letter lent by Mrs. Arthur J. Walter, Adrian, Missouri.

4. "(I am more) confident now (of suc)ceeding as a painter t(han) I was before I (came) here, I design next winter to try (what) I can do in the South and wherever I (may) be, I am determined to use every exertion to become distinguished in the profession which I have adopted." From other fragments of the letter it may be inferred that Bingham expected by the first of April to be financially able to marry, and he expressed the supposition that the wedding, which they once expected to have in Franklin, will "then, at last," take place in Boonville.—Rusk, *op. cit.*, p. 22. Quoted from letter lent the author by Mrs. Arthur J. Walter, Adrian, Missouri. The portions in parentheses are missing in the mutilated original letter.

5. "His extreme poverty made it necessary for him to undergo, literally, the proverbial hardships of the young artist. During his stay in the city he slept rolled up in a blanket in an unfinished attic."—Rusk, *op. cit.*, p. 21.

6. See p. 18.

7. See p. 3.

8. Rollins, *op. cit.*, p. 466.

9. *Ibid.*, p. 468.

10. Fern Helen Rusk has identified these early portraits as Mr. Josiah Lamme and Mrs. Josiah Lamme and son. Mr. C. B. Rollins, who owns the latter portrait, reports the names to be Mr. David Steel Lamme, and Mrs. David Steel Lamme and son.

11. Rogers, Meyric R., *Bulletin of the City Art Museum of St. Louis*, XIX, No. 2 (April, 1934), 17–18.

THE EASTERN INFLUENCE

1. "In 1838, he spent three months in Philadelphia, and obtained a little knowledge of color by looking at pictures which before he had no opportunity of studying."—*Columbia Statesman*, August 31, 1849. The writer has corresponded with Julian P. Boyd of the Pennsylvania Historical Society in Philadelphia, but no further information was available concerning Bingham's stay there in 1837.

2. Rusk, *op. cit.*, p. 25.

3. Rogers, *op. cit.*, p. 18.

4. Rollins, *op. cit.*, p. 469.

THE POLITICAL INFLUENCE

1. Rollins, *op. cit.*, p. 469.

2. Switzler, *History of Missouri*, p. 256.

3. Rollins, *op. cit.*, p. 469.

4. Pope, *op. cit.*, p. 15.

5. Conversation with Dr. John Pickard, onetime Professor of Art, University of Missouri.

6. Musick, *op. cit.*, p. 14.

7. See p. 38.

8. Rusk, *op. cit.*, pp. 27–28, quoting from Colonel R. B. Price, Columbia, friend of the artist.

9. Rollins, *op. cit.*, p. 464.

10.   "Washington Feb 21, 1841

". . . Though I have a painting room in the capitol, I know less of the proceedings of Congress than if I were in Missouri, the fact is I am no politician here, and as the great question of the ability of the people to control their rulers is settled for the present, I am so well satisfied with the result, that the Locos have my leave to do their worst during the brief period of their power. . . .

"I am a painter and desire to be nothing else, and unless another corrupt dynasty, like the one that has just been overthrown, shall again arouse the energy of the whole people in behalf of a suffering country, I shall be content to pursue the quiet tenor of a painters life, contending only for the smiles of the graces, while the great world may jog along as it pleases. . . ."

11. It evidently became "necessary" soon after this date. See p. 39.

12. Pope, *op. cit.*, p. 15.

13. Rollins, *op. cit.*, p. 471.

14. "Bingham is said to have painted a host of celebrities while there, among them Webster, Clay, Walker, Breckenridge, Andrew Jackson, Calhoun, Buchanan, Van Buren, John Howard Payne, and John Quincy Adams."—Rusk, *op. cit.*, p. 29.

15. See p. 14.

16. Rollins, *op. cit.*, p. 471.

THE GENRE PAINTINGS

1. "It was in Washington City in 1844 that Bingham painted 'Jolly Flatboatmen,' his first genre canvas. This painting was purchased in 1845 by the American Art Union, and an engraving of it appeared as the frontispiece of their Journal for 1845 as the best picture of the kind that had appeared in this country the year before. It gave Bingham a wide reputation among eastern artists."—Rollins, *op. cit.*, p. 472.

2. "This American Art Union was an organization incorporated by the Legislature of New York, which had for its purpose the promotion of Fine Arts in the

United States, the encouragement of native artists and the diffusion of American art through the country. Membership was obtained upon the payment of five dollars, and these fees were used to pay for engravings of one or more American paintings and to purchase as many works of art as possible in both painting and sculpture by native or resident artists. (The Art Union bought only pictures exhibited at its gallery, 497 Broadway, New York, and approved by a committee.) Each member received at least one engraving in the year, and every five-dollar share he owned also gave him a chance of obtaining works in painting and sculpture, which were distributed by lot. Editors of the leading papers all over the country were made honorary secretaries, and shares could be purchased through them. In 1849 the membership numbered more than ten thousand, and the Union was planning a distribution of Cole's *Youth*, the second in his series of the *Voyage of Life*, and also a volume of etchings illustrating Irving's tale of the Legend of Sleepy Hollow."—*Missouri Statesman*, July 6, 1849.

3. Rollins, *op. cit.*, p. 472.

4. Mr. C. B. Rollins validates this statement.

5. American Art Union *Transactions* for 1847, No. I, p. 32.

6. See p. 37.

7. See p. 91 ff.

8. The writer has attempted to examine or obtain information about the Mastin paintings, *Jolly Flatboatmen* and *Washington Crossing the Delaware*. However, because of an unfortunate experience suffered at some early date when they lent their pictures, the Mastins were not willing to show their paintings.

9. Rusk, *op. cit.*, p. 32, names *Fur Traders Descending the Missouri* as the first genre picture by Bingham. This is probably incorrect, for Mr. C. B. Rollins, when questioned concerning this difference of opinion, stated that he had got the material upon which he based his article from letters written by Bingham to Rollins, which are now unfortunately no longer in existence. Mr. Rollins also agrees with the writer that the so-called genre period in the painting of Bingham began earlier than 1844. He feels that it is safe to assume that Bingham received his inspiration to do genre in Philadelphia. When he returned to Missouri and joined the political discussions of 1840 the artist began making his genre sketches as stated previously in this account. Thus, *Jolly Flatboatmen*, as well as *Fur Traders Descending the Missouri*, may well have been conceived and executed any time between 1840 and 1844.

10. Rogers, *George Caleb Bingham, The Missouri Artist*, p. 20.

11. An interesting, amusingly flamboyant account of the assemblies, at which the banners were challengingly flaunted, may be entertaining:

"The 10th and 11th days of October, 1844, were days long to be remembered by the gallant Whigs of Missouri and will be referred to in future as the days on which assembled in our city the most glorious convention that our State has ever witnessed. . . . The procession . . . then the immense delegation from Howard, bearing a most splendid banner, on one side of which our noble champion is represented advocating the 'American System.' 'All the great interests' of America are here represented. On one hand is a fortress with our National Flag waving above it; on the other, and to the rearward is the ocean, crowded with shipping, and farther in the front is a farmer with his plough, a railroad, a number of dingy manufacturing establishments, the capitol and other national buildings, while Mr. Clay, with his hands extended towards them, exclaims in his own impressive manner, 'All these great interests are confided to the protection and care of government!' The portrait of Mr. Clay as well as the entire picture is an admirable specimen of painting, and both as to design and execution is highly creditable to the artist. On the reverse side of the banner is represented a prairie, in its uncultivated state, with a herd of buffalo roving across it. . . .

"And finally came the Ashland Club—composed of the young men of Boonville, and the Boonville Juvenile Clay Club. The Ashland Club bore decidedly the most beautiful banner we have ever seen. On one side was represented the plain, unostentatious, but noble farmer of Ashland on his farm; on the reverse side is an Eagle perched high on a firm, immovable rock. The banner is without letters—save the name of the club—the devices alone being sufficiently significant. The Juvenile Club also bore a most beautiful banner; on one side of which is represented a mill boy riding merrily through the slashes of Hanover to mill; on the reverse side is a little fellow carving the name of Henry Clay. A mere description of the devices on these banners, however, conveys no idea of their real beauty. They, as also the Howard banner, were painted by Mr. Bingham, a noble young artist of this city."
—*Boonville Observer*, October 15, 1844.

12. "Last fall I was in New Franklin, Howard county, and met Mr. George C. Edwards, an old citizen. I inquired of him if by any chance he knew anything of those banners. He told me he was thoroughly familiar with them and that a few years before, they had been destroyed by fire when the store of Mr. Alsop in New Franklin, where the banners were hanging, burned."—Rollins, *op. cit.*, p. 471.

13. "Saline.—Geo. C. Bingham, Esq., the celebrated artist, is the whig candidate for the Legislature in Saline county. Mr. Bingham if elected, and we doubt not that he will be, will prove an able and faithful representative. We congratulate the whigs on having chosen a candidate who commands the respect of all parties; and who enjoys the confidence, and will receive the undivided support of his own. Mr. Bingham is well armed at all points to meet any gentleman who may be chosen to oppose him; intimately acquainted with the political history of his country, a cogent reasoner, and a handsome speaker. He is *as true* to nature too, in his portraitures of Locofocoism, as of the human face divine."—*Boonville Observer*, June 24, 1846.

14. Rollins, *op. cit.*, p. 472.

15. Bingham, "Art, the Ideal of Art and the Utility of Art," University of Missouri *Public Lectures*, p. 314.

16. *Order No. 11.*

17. "Speech of GEORGE C. BINGHAM, of Saline County, Delivered in the House of Representatives of the Missouri Legislature, Thursday, December 17th, 1846, in reply to Attorney General B. F. Stringfellow, the counsel for Mr. Sappington, who contested the seat of Mr. Bingham.

"Mr. Bingham rose and spoke in substance as follows:

"Mr. Speaker: Having passed the greater portion of my life since I arrive at the state of manhood, in the pursuit of a quiet and peaceful profession, I am constrained to confess, that the position in which I now find myself placed, is anything but an enviable one. But I find consolation in the fact, that I am occupying the post which duty assigns me.—I am here, not only to defend my own rights, but the rights of the honored constituency whose representative I claim to be; and so far as my abilities shall enable me, I will persevere in the discharge of that duty, in despite of my natural repugnance to the task, or the obstacles that are thrown in my path.

"In this contest, sir, I have nothing to guide me but the dictates of common sense, and nothing to sustain me but truth; while upon the opposite side, I find pitted against me a gentleman whose office at least should require the highest legal abilities of the State, and who if we are to credit his own statements, is certainly no ordinary man. For he graciously informs this House, that although, during the preliminary investigation of this case before the committee, he frequently found himself opposed to six lawyers, he was not disposed to surrender his opinion in deference to them all! I behold towering up before me a legal Colossus, and it may seem strange to this House, that one so weak and feeble as myself does not cower in such a presence, and shrink back dismayed from such an unequal conflict!

"But in the midst of my profound humiliation, my mind fortunately reverts to a story contained in the good old book, which our mothers read to us in the days of our childhood, and which perhaps a small portion of this House may still remember. The story to which I allude is that one Goliah of Gath, whose immense physical stature might justly be compared to the legal dimensions of our Attorney General, fell beneath a pebble, slung from the arm of a stripling shepherd.

"It is true sir, that my arm may not be strong with the sinews which gave energy to that of the youthful David, but the skull of the giant with whom I contend, may not perhaps prove so hard as that of the Philistine. I do not therefore entirely despair of being able to lodge in the brain of this modern Goliah, a few of those shining pebbles, which may be picked up, even by an unskillful hand, from the borders of the ever-flowing rivulets of truth. . . .

"*I illegally procured the certificate of my election!* Why, sir, I am not a politician by trade; I am not one of those whose sole study it is to enrich themselves by the spoils and emoluments of office, and consequently familiar with all the wiles and windings of political intrigue! I have ever been, and expect ever hereafter to remain, one of the people; to be affected by the changes and mutations of parties and of policy, only as my interest is identified or connected with that of the great mass

[160]

of the people themselves."—*Boonville Observer*, March 11, 1847.

18. Rusk, *op. cit.*, p. 37.

19. Mr. C. B. Rollins remembers distinctly a painting of this subject matter, and it may be this one to which the American Art Union *Transactions* refer.

20. Rogers, *George Caleb Bingham, The Missouri Artist*, p. 11.

21. *St. Louis Republican*, April 12, 1847.

22. Rusk, *op. cit.*, p. 41.

23. Pope, *op. cit.*, p. 15.

24. Rusk, *op. cit.*, p. 47.

25. Simonds, May, "A Pioneer Painter," *American Illustrated Methodist Magazine*, VIII, October, 1902.

26. Rusk, *op. cit.*, pp. 45–46, quoting from the *Kansas City Star*, October 6, 1901.

27. *Bulletin* of the American Art Union, August, 1849.

28. American Art Union *Transactions*, 1849, No. 218, p. 50.

29. American Art Union *Transactions*, 1849, No. 241, p. 51.

30. American Art Union *Transactions*, 1849, No. 196, p. 49.

31. Bingham, *op. cit.*, pp. 312–324.

32. *Columbia Statesman*, August 31, 1849.

33. *Missouri Statesman*, September 28, 1849.

34. "The Lathrop Portrait.—The meeting of the ladies at the Court House on Friday evening was large—Mrs. Philips presiding. A committee of twenty-five was appointed to accept the Portrait of President Lathrop (painted and tendered by G. C. Bingham) and to ask the Board of Curators to have it hung in the Chapel of the University. The proceedings of the Board and the correspondence touching the subject we will publish hereafter."—*Columbia Statesman*, December 27, 1850.

35. Neff, L. J. B. unpublished "Sketch of Bingham."

36. *Bulletin* of the American Art Union, 1850, p. 64 ff.

37. "A whole legend has sprung up around the bellicose personage of Mike Fink, one of the most celebrated of these inland navigators. He is said to have proclaimed himself in words which combined braggadocio and fact: 'I'm a Salt River Rorer! I'm chuck full of fight and I love the wimmin!' He was so expert with the rifle that in matches for beef, such as Bingham has painted, he was always awarded the 'fifth quarter,' that is, the hide and tallow, on condition that he keep out of the competition."—Musick, *op. cit.*, p. 14.

38. Rusk, *op. cit.*

39. *Ibid.*, p. 50, quoting from *Supplementary Bulletin*, December, 1851, and December, 1852.

40. *Ibid.*, p. 51, quoting from the *Bulletin* of the American Art Union, May-December, 1851, Nos. 52, 120, 130, 152, 173; *Supplementary Bulletin*, December, 1852, p. 3 ff., Nos. 41, 53, 162, 194, 221, 352.

41. Any number of logical analyses would be plausible here. On the one hand, there might have been but one painting, *Fishing on the Mississippi*, even if the

measurements of that painting are represented to be 36 x 26, while the Rockhill Nelson painting is 28¼ x 35⅞. Some error in recording the measurements may have been committed by the Art Union, or in measuring they may have included the frame. Anyway, it is a fact that the description of *Fishing on the Mississippi* fits exactly the painting *Fishing on the Missouri*.

42. See p. 37.

43. Information from Mrs. Louise Burroughs, Metropolitan Museum of Art.

44. This might refer to *In a Quandary*.

45. Possibly *Canvassing for a Vote*. Musick, *op. cit.*, pp. 21–22.

46. "An examination of the picture will show the 'ghosting' of the first painting now visible owing to the increasing transparency of oil pigment with age. This apparently confirms the opinion that the picture was considerably repainted after the lithograph was made, for the latter shows a quite different treatment of the landscape in a somewhat higher key. Though the painting is, of course, an imaginary composition, there is evidence in the sketches that the most important figures were carefully studied from posed models."—Musick, *op. cit.*, p. 21.

47. *Ibid.*

48. Rusk, *op. cit.*, pp. 52–53.

49. See pp. 73–74 for another portion of the letter.

50. *Missouri Statesman*, May 23, 1851.

51. *Courier-Journal*, Louisville, Kentucky, May 11, 1923.

52. "Modern Museum Holds Exhibition of Bingham's Art," Mary Morsell, Editor, *The Art News*, February 2, 1935, p. 6.

53. Because a sufficient number of the paintings have been reproduced here in color, it seems unnecessary to spend more words upon Bingham's color methods. The reader is urged to make a careful study of the colored plates.

54. Pope, *op. cit.*, p. 15.

55. It is interesting to note that there is a striking similarity between Bingham's *County Election* and *The Election—Canvassing for a Vote*, II, by William Hogarth.

56. Childs, *op. cit.*, p. 598.

57. Rollins, C. B.

58. John D. Whiting, illustrator, once remarked to the writer that an observant draughtsman should be able to show, by drawing merely the shoes of an individual, the social scale of the wearer. He went further to say that he had often noticed the differences between the footwear of a college president and that of an assistant professor. It wears in different places.

59. Rollins, C. B.

60. Rusk, *op. cit.*, p. 54, quoting from the New York *Mirror*, copied in the *Missouri Statesman*, September 10, 1852.

61. "The Jolly Flatboatmen is one exception. When asked why he had failed to represent one here he replied, 'I have not, the dog is in the hold.' "—Rusk, *op. cit.*, p. 97, quoting Col. R. B. Price.

62. Rollins, C. B.

63. Mr. C. B. Rollins concurs in this opinion.

64. Simonds, May, "A Pioneer Painter," *American Illustrated Methodist Magazine*, VIII, October, 1902.

65. One of these engravings, washed with water color, is now in the private collection of Mr. C. B. Rollins, Sr., of Columbia, Missouri.

66. Rusk, *op. cit.*, p. 59.

67. For remainder of letter see p. 77–78.

68. Rollins, *op. cit.*, p. 473.

69. For beginning of letter see p. 76.

70. A typical Renaissance device in composing. The same "stage" scheme can be found in many 18th century Italian paintings, Canaletto's for example.

71. Rollins, C. B.

72. Rollins, C. B.

73. What these pictures were, we do not know.

74. This newspaper notice states that "Bingham's County Election is on the market."

"Mr. Bingham has had his unrivalled painting, THE COUNTY ELECTION, engraved in Sartain's best style, and it is now ready for delivery. Messrs. Nanson & Bartholow are in receipt of several of the engravings, and will deliver them to all subscribers. The engraving is 22 by 30 inches, and there is over one hundred figures distinctly portrayed. Persons who have been in the habit of attending any of our elections will at once catch the design, and almost read the thoughts of different persons portrayed in the group. Mr. B. is one of our own people, and we are sure this great work of his will be largely called for. In conception and execution it takes rank among the best productions, of art.

"The original price of subscription is $10. Mr. B. has frames and glass which he furnishes to such subscribers as may desire them, at cost, which will make the price of the engraving, in a tasty frame, covered by good glass, $16.50."–*Glasgow Weekly Times*, November 23, 1854.

75. Bingham had probably been away on a brief trip—perhaps to Louisville, Kentucky.

76. In a letter written in 1902 by Rollins Bingham, son of the artist, it is stated that the painting purchased by Mr. Peters for $200 at the administrator's sale in 1893, is a replica and that the one in the Mercantile Library is the original.

77. Pope, *op. cit.*, pp. 15–16.

THE LATE WORK AND POLITICAL LIFE

1. Rusk, *op. cit.*, p. 64, reports the time to be eighteen years. Her informer, a Mrs. Birch, a contemporary friend of the artist, must have been mistaken, however, for Bingham in a letter to Rollins from Philadelphia, January 7, 1872, writes:

". . . He (Sartain) seems quite anxious to engrave my picture of 'Washington Crossing the Delaware' which is now finished. . . ."

2. See note 8 on "The Genre Paintings."

3. Leutze is mentioned by Bingham in the letter on p. 85; also mentioned in Rusk, *op. cit.*, p. 65.

4. Thomas Benton has said, in conversation with the writer, that many artists are incapable of working without basing the structures rather specifically upon object matter observed. Bingham, he thinks, is one of them.

5. To realize fully how thoroughly Bingham subscribed to this philosophy the reader should turn to pp. 120 ff. to examine the address prepared by the artist for presentation before the student body and faculty of the University of Missouri, March 1, 1879.

6. "The school that had grown up in this center was of a literary character, caring little for artistic color or atmosphere, but laying stress upon the arrangement of stage scenes to make compositions that would tell stories. So we readily see why Bingham was attracted to it. His love of sincere, simple life, however, saved him from the insipid, sentimental work characteristic of such leading members of the school as Lessing and Hildebrant."—Rusk, *op. cit.*, p. 65.

7. There is no available evidence to prove that this contemplated painting was ever done.

8. See pp. 35 ff.

9. Childs, *op. cit.*, p. 598.

10. Pope, *op. cit.*, p. 16.

11. See pp. 35 ff.

12. Rusk, *op. cit.*, p. 69, quoting from Mrs. Helen R. Parsons.

13. Rollins, *op. cit.*, p. 478.

14. February 5, 1859.

15. Rusk, *op. cit.*, p. 70.

16. Rollins, *op. cit.*, p. 478.

17. January 12, 1861.

18. Viles, *A History of Missouri*, p. 236.

19. Rusk, pp. 77–78. Letter lent by Mrs. Arthur J. Walter, Adrian, Missouri.

20. "Bingham served his term as State Treasurer, which lasted till 1865, with the strictest integrity during a time when the confusion and excitement of war troubles made money matters very uncertain and the acquisition of money by officials in positions of trust very easy; particularly did the treasurer's office offer every chance for such, without the necessity of stooping to absolute robbery. The state had issued millions of dollars in 'Union Defense Warrants' which bore interest at the rate of six per cent per annum, and a special tax was levied to raise funds for the redemption of the warrants, which were made redeemable at the State Treasurer's office. At the time Bingham was redeeming these, two years after they had been issued, they depreciated to twenty-five cents below par, which added to the

interest would amount to thirty-seven cents on the dollar. Had Bingham wished to make a fortune from these, he could have done it without robbing the State Treasury of anything. St. Louis banks urged him to do it, offering to furnish all the money necessary and divide the profits with him; but he was above taking advantage of the people because of the opportunity which the turbulent time offered. The treasury kept for convenience and safety large sums of money in a St. Louis bank. One deposit Bingham himself had loaded into an ox-cart and taken there by night at a time when it was feared that the capital city might be attacked by the Confederates under General Sterling Price. After Bingham had finished his work as treasurer and had straightened out his accounts to the perfect satisfaction of the government, the St. Louis bank sent him a statement to the effect that it was indebted to him twenty-seven thousand dollars in the form of a deposit subject to his order. Bingham wrote to the bank that it was a mistake; but the reply came that the amount was due him. So he went with his bookkeeper to St. Louis and after days of investigation proved to the bank that there was nothing due him either as State Treasurer or privately."—Rusk, Fern Helen, *op. cit.*, pp. 81–82, from Louella S. Vincent.

21. Rollins, *op. cit.*, p. 480.

22. "Though a staunch Unionist, our artist was as relentless in his denunciation of what he considered unjust acts on the part of men allied with his party as of those by members of the opposition. . . . There were during the early part of the war bands of robbers and murderers who continually made plundering raids from Kansas over into the border counties of Missouri. This trouble had become so serious that the commanding officers deemed speedy and decisive measures necessary to stop it. Some thought the only means would be to lay waste the border so that the source of shelter and subsistence for the marauding bands should be cut off. So Brigadier-General Ewing, who was in command of the military district of 'the Border,' issued an order on the twenty-fifth of August, 1863, commanding the removal of all the inhabitants of that district, except those in certain localities, within fifteen days. Only those who should establish their loyalty were to be allowed to go to military stations in the district. As far as possible, grain and hay were to be taken to the stations, and that which was beyond reach was to be burned. This order affected several counties and parts of counties, and Unionists suffered along with the rest at the hands of many of the officers and others pretending to be officers who executed the order. Bingham felt that such a severe measure was not necessary. He said that 'it did, indeed, put an end to the predatory raids of Kansas red-legs and jayhawkers by surrendering to them all that they coveted, leaving nothing that could further excite their cupidity, but it gave up the country to bushwhackers, who, until the close of the war, continued to stop the stages and rob the mails and passengers; and no one wearing the federal uniform dared to risk his life within the desolated district.' This order, together with several other disgraceful affairs for which Bingham believed Ewing to be responsible, made the

artist Ewing's bitter enemy."—Rusk, *op. cit.*, pp. 82–83.

23. *Jefferson City Weekly People's Tribune*, December 23, 1868.

24. *St. Louis Missouri Republican*, March 17, 1869.

25. Crittenden, *The Crittenden Memoirs*, p. 342.

26. *Missouri Statesman*, July 6, 1866.

27. Smith, *op. cit.*, p. 68.

28. Rusk, *op. cit.*, pp. 93–94.

29. Smith, *op. cit.*, pp. 93–94.

30. "Some sketches owned by Mr. C. B. Rollins, which were done by Bingham while he was in Major Rollins' home, show little represented in his work elsewhere, the academic nude and the religious. We have found academic treatment before, and there is a nude child in *The Thread of Life*. But these seem to have been suggested by Giorgione's *Venus*, a standing nude in the attitude of the *Venus de Medici* and a seated one in almost the same attitude. These figures are rather carefully drawn, but they are too heavy, coarse, and clumsy in proportions. The religious subject represents *Christ and Mary in the Garden*. Mary assumes almost the same posture as one of the figures in *Order No. 11*; she kneels before Christ with her arms raised in supplication and her face full of yearning. Christ's face is not so good; he looks down upon Mary with an amiable but not essentially loving or devout expression. The extremities are poorly drawn, and the drapery appears to have given trouble; it is much worked over with hesitating strokes and is not good at last. A cow grazing and, particularly, an old woman reading, and a number of heads of men are the best things among these sketches. Less labored in finish, they appear to have been dashed off rapidly, and with a few strokes the character is plainly expressed. Some of the heads are much like work in the St. Louis Mercantile Library sketchbook, though less carefully finished."—Rusk, *op. cit.*, p. 95.

31. "It is a large picture, about three and a half by five feet. The artist has chosen a view which brings the highest point of the peak a little to the left of the center of the picture. The sun is pouring a flood of light upon the scene in the foreground, except for a few spots where it is cut off by the fleecy clouds. Down over the rocks at the right flows a stream of water, bubbling and foaming in little cascades, while in the quieter parts the rocks are mirrored on its surface. There is some vegetation visible, particularly at the left; as we should expect in such bare, bleak surroundings. At the left, on a rock among the trees in a path of sunlight sits an Indian, quietly resting, with a rifle in his hand and feathers in his hair. His form is not made conspicuous, no more so than one of the trees. In spite of all the interest in the foreground, the lofty snow-capped peak towering behind it dominates the picture. In painting this canvas, as well as his other landscapes, the artist, we are told, made many sketches from nature in pencil and oil, representing the scene in the varying effects of atmosphere, and finally from these sketches he painted the pictures in his studio. Portfolios containing a great many sketches were in existence a short time before the artist's death; but they have since been destroyed or lost.

Probably the *Pike's Peak*, two and a half by four and a half feet, owned by Mr. R. S. Thomas of Blue Springs, was one of the studies for the large canvas."—Rusk, *op. cit.*, pp. 94–95.

32. Rusk, *op. cit.*, p. 97, states that these pictures might be the same known to us as *Moonlight View*, *Winter Scene* and *Landscape Views*. The first is owned by Mr. R. W. Thomas, Kansas City, and the latter two, by Mr. R. S. Thomas, Blue Springs, Missouri.

33. See note 10 on "The Early Work."

34. Rusk, *op. cit.*, p. 97.

35. Mr. C. B. Rollins.

THE LAST YEARS

1. *Jefferson City Daily Tribune*, March 4, 1876, from the *Saline County Progress*.

2.   "Washington, D. C. April 13,
                                                    1876

". . . As to your dear little friend Vinnie my wife had been in advance of you in the request that I would avail myself of the leisure forced upon me here, to paint her portrait. As she has in her possession a portrait of herself painted by the distinguished artist Healy which I am forced to regard as a failure, I hesitated to comply with my wife's request fearing that where such generally recognized ability had failed I might fail also. As the dear little woman, however, expressed her willingness to risk the result, I commenced the work in her own studio. It is now nearly completed, and I am gratified in knowing that it gives satisfaction to herself, family and those who rank as her best friends. Voorhees of Indiana appears chief of these last. He is delighted with the portrait and claims the honor of contributing to it an appropriate frame. I represent her in her simple working costume, as engaged in modelling the bust of President Lincoln. I can be of no service to her in directing her art studies. Her taste is refined and most exquisite. I can see from her works that she has closely studied the immortal remains of Greek art as handed to us from the days of Pericles. These works furnish the proper school for her, and she has already availed herself, in an eminent degree, of the advantages which they afford. I am not at all surprised that she has excited the envy of contemporary artists in her own department. Few of them can claim to be her equals and in some respects she is ahead of them all. . . ."

3. Rusk, *op. cit.*, p. 102.

4. "Hon. Geo. C. Bingham has entered upon his duties at the State University as Professor of the School of Art."—*Boonville Weekly Eagle*, October 12, 1877.

5. This amusing account may be of interest:
          "Marriage of Genl. Geo. C. Bingham to Mrs. Lykins.
"The marriage of Gen. George C. Bingham and Mrs. Johnston Lykins was solemnized yesterday morning at 8 o'clock. The ceremony was performed by the

Rev. Mr. Chamblis, of this city, in the parlors of the Lykins Institute or Female Academy, about a mile south of the city limits. Here, in the midst of a rural region unsurpassed for the beauty of its surroundings a very quiet little wedding was enacted. The parlors in which the interesting ceremonies that were to unite culture and taste, to artistic honors and ability, were to take place, had been festooned with fragrant flowers from the home conservatory, intermingled with gracefully-hanging evergreen boughs. Vases of most beautiful fuchias in full bloom filled the corners of the rooms. Hanging from the centre of the ceiling in the front parlor, over the heads of the friends there gathered, was a beautiful evergreen wreath; from the centre of the ceiling of the back parlor, under which stood the high contracting parties, was a magnificent wedding bell, fully three feet across, and duly proportioned, constructed of the sombre bloom of the smoke tree, ornamented with evergreens and flowers, and fragrant with heliotrope and honeysuckle. As the pair stood there, he the successful artist, with a national reputation, whose well-wielded brush has painted pictures that shall live forever, and she the acknowledged equal in taste, aesthetic culture and executive ability, the scene was not joyous, but impressive. Pastor Chambliss, in a few well-chosen words, referred to God's beneficence in establishing for man the institution of marriage, and then, after a brief invocation, and after having exacted from them the usual promise to 'love, cherish and honor,' pronounced Gen. Geo. C. Bingham, and she who had been so long Mrs. Mattie Lykins, husband and wife. The congratulations were prompt and hearty, all the friends but one being younger than the newly married couple. At 9 o'clock a most bountiful breakfast was partaken of by the assembled guests. To say that the repast was equal to a royal feast would not do justice to the occasion; its real and true description would be impossible. A fine array of silver-ware, glass ware and well-filled albums, as presents from friends, occupied a table in the parlors.

"At 10 o'clock, the General and wife, accompanied by a few friends, were driven to the depot, and took the cars for Denver, to spend a few weeks among the magnificent scenery of Colorado.

"General George C. Bingham is well known throughout the State as the Adjutant General of Missouri during Governor Hardin's administration. He has also won for himself a wide reputation as an artist. Some of his paintings have even acquired a national celebrity. Mrs. Bingham is a lady widely and favorably known in Western Missouri, as the founder of the Orphan Home for Confederate soldiers' children, which institution she, with the assistance of other benevolent ladies, established some years ago. When the State of Missouri made an appropriation for the establishment of an Orphans' Home at Kansas City, the Lykins' Orphan Home was purchased and a new building erected. It was there where the ceremony of yesterday took place.

"The newly married pair carry with them on their western pleasure tour the heartiest good wishes and congratulations of a large host of Missouri friends.— K. C. Times, 19th."

THE MAN

1. Rollins, *op. cit.*, p. 483.

2. Mr. C. B. Rollins believes this portrait to have been painted about the year 1877. It is possible that the artist completed it with the intention of presenting it to Mrs. Mattie Lykins, whom he married in June of the following year. However, there seems to be no evidence to date the picture exactly.

3. The tragic mental suffering and death of his second wife gave Bingham such agony that he wrote to his Columbia friend letters which, because of their heart revealing confidence, Mr. C. B. Rollins has requested should not yet be published. These intimate pages have been sealed and put away until some distant time when "added years will have put sufficient distance between the artist and his immediate family and friends that they can be read with impersonal understanding." Immediately following the death of Mrs. Bingham, the son, Rollins Bingham, became afflicted by a mental trouble which turned him against his father. The great soul of the father gave expression to his grief in letters to Mr. Rollins which are noble in their fortitude.

4. Rollins, *op. cit.*, pp. 463–464.

5. *Ibid.*, pp. 464–465.

6. *Ibid.*, p. 465.

7. *Ibid.*, p. 466.

8. *Ibid.*, p. 483.

9. From the *Sentinal-Tribune*, Kansas City, July 10, 1879.

10. From a clipping in the scrapbook of Mr. C. B. Rollins. He is not able to place the source exactly, but knows that he got it from a Kansas City paper.

THE BINGHAM REVIVAL: AN EVALUATION

1. The place Benton is given in the field of modern American art by Thomas Craven, and the esteem in which Bingham is held by such an authority as Meyric R. Rogers, are good evidence.

2. Childs, *op. cit.*, p. 595.

3. Mrs. Louise J. Bingham Neff, unpublished "Sketch of Bingham"; Miss May Simonds, unpublished "Sketch of Bingham's Life"; Mrs. Helen R. Parsons, an article, "Missouri's Greatest Painter."

4. Childs, *op. cit.*, p. 595.

5. See note 23 on "Historical Background in Missouri."

6. Rusk, *op. cit.*, p. 117.

THE paintings referred to are here catalogued and listed as to their owner-ship and size, whenever this information could be obtained.

[170]